Celebrating CIGARS

Anwer Bati

First published in Great Britain in 2004 by
Duncan Petersen Publishing Ltd,
31 Ceylon Road, London W14 OPY

ISBN 1-903301-39-4

Editorial director Andrew Duncan
Designers Picthall and Gunzi; David Fordham
Editor Sophie Page
Picture research Tamara Grosvenor and Frances Vargo
Studio photography by Geoff Dann

Colour reproduction by the Colour House, London
Printed by Polygraf Print, Slovakia

Foreword

My first book on hand made cigars, *The Cigar Companion*, became the world's best-selling title on the subject. It also contributed to the 1990s cigar boom by helping readers become knowledgeable about what they were buying. I later wrote two other books which also sold internationally: *The Essential Cigar*, a beginners' guide, and *The Complete Cigar Book*. The latter was very comprehensive, but space didn't allow as much coverage of individual brands as I would have liked. *Celebrating Cigars*, on the other hand, not only contains more information about the brands listed in it than any other book, but its large format also means that there are more cigars illustrated (full-size at that) than ever before. I hope this book will add to your enjoyment, and tell you all you need to know about your favourite brands - as well as many other aspects of the world of cigars.

Anwer Bati

Contents

Cigar History
8-39

Making Cigars
40-63

Cigar Directory
64-161

Cigar Lists
162-171

Cigar Art and Accessories
172-187

Cigar People
188-205

Index
206-208

The History of
CIGARS

CIGARS AS WE KNOW THEM – with their expert construction, careful blending,
and subtle aromas – have existed for less than 200 years. But tobacco
has been cultivated for at least a millenium, so that the development of today's cigars
has been a slow process – their history dramatically linked to wars,
the rise and fall of empires and the flow of international trade.

*H*OW AND WHERE cigars, or something like them, first came to be made or smoked is a matter of conjecture. Indeed, nobody really knows. But we're on firmer ground with the cultivation of tobacco. Historians agree that the most likely place where tobacco was first deliberately grown was Central America, probably by the Maya of the Yucatan peninsula, now part of Mexico. The area is, perhaps significantly, only a couple of hundred kilometres from the island of Cuba.

The Maya were famed not only for their great cities and skill at mathematics, but also for their competence in agriculture. Their civilization spread over southern Mexico, Guatemala, Belize and Honduras. A fragment of Guatemalan pottery dating from the 10th Century – by which time Mayan culture was firmly in decline – shows a man smoking what appears to be a bundle of tobacco leaves held together by twine or string. It is possibly the forerunner of the cigar. But Mayan civilization was more than two thousand years old by then, and we don't know if this was a current fashion, or an ancient custom.

Central and South America also provides evidence of tobacco being smoked by peoples other than the Maya. We know that the pre-Columbian inhabitants used to smoke crushed tobacco wrapped by corn or other plant leaves: a form closer to the cigarette than the cigar. And the Aztecs, whose power in Mexico reached its peak in the 15th Century, used to smoke tobacco essentially in pipe form – stuffed in hollow reeds or cane. Indeed tobacco seems to have been smoked in many parts of the American continent partly, it is thought, because of the collapse of Mayan civilization (around 900 AD) – which resulted in widespread migration within the continent, and quite conceivably to Cuba. Tobacco cultivation spread, the theory is, as the Maya migrated. The native Americans of what is now the United States, for instance, smoked tobacco in long pipes. Thomas Hariot, in his *A Briefe and True Report of the New Found Land of Viginia* (1588), records the local native Americans drying tobacco leaves and powdering them: 'they take the fume or smoke thereof by sucking it through pipes made of clay into their stomach and head . . . it is of so precious estimation amongst them, that they think their gods are marvelously delighted . . . sometime they make hallowed fires and cast some of the powder therein . . . to pacify their gods'.

So, it seems that tobacco was smoked in several different ways (it was also chewed and taken as an infusion). Another variation was noted in 1535 by Gonzalo

Fernandez de Oviedo, in his *Natural History of the West Indies*, where he mentions that, 'the Indians used a Y-shaped tube, putting the two ends of the fork up their nostrils and the tube in the burning grasses.' And it was as likely to have been smoked for medicinal and ritual or religious reasons – seen by some as a way of communing with the gods – as it was for pleasure.

EUROPE DISCOVERS TOBACCO

BUT ALTHOUGH we know tobacco was smoked in different forms in America at least a thousand years ago – and very possibly for much longer, the plant was unknown to the rest of the world until Christopher Columbus's attempt to find a new route to India and China led to his encounter with the New World.

Even though Columbus led the expedition, precisely who can claim to have 'discovered' tobacco is also unclear, but the best claimants are Rodrigo de Jerez and Luis de Torres. Columbus landed in Cuba on 28th October, 1492. He didn't actually know where he was, but is reported to have thought he was in China. The following month, he sent two men – de Jerez, and de Torres – to inspect the interior of the island. They returned with stories of their meetings with the local Taino Indians. The Tainos, they said, 'had torches in their hands and certain herbs to breathe in the smoke, dried herbs enclosed in a certain

Above THE GENOA-BORN EXPLORER CHRISTOPHER
COLUMBUS (*A NON SMOKER*) OFFERS A SWEETNER TO
NATIVE CENTRAL AMERICANS.

leaf, also dried . . . lit on one end, while on the other, they were drawing or sucking, breathing in that smoke, with which they numb their flesh and which is almost intoxicating, and in this way they say they never feel fatigue.' These crude cigars consisted of twisted tobacco leaves rolled in a corn, palm or plantain leaf, and Rodigo de Jerez was probably the first European to smoke them.

The Taino certainly used the word 'tobacco', or *tobaga*, but nobody's sure whether it referred to the leaf, the smoke or the act or method of smoking. But it is possible that the Taino actually called the leaf *cojoba* or *cohiba,* the name now given to one of Cuba's most famous brands. If that's true, it suggests that 'tobacco' was the word for smoking. Even so, some have suggested that tobacco was a corruption of the name of the Caribbean island of Tobago or the Mexican province of Tabasco.

Who first brought tobacco to the Old World is also a matter of dispute, but it is clear that tobacco must have been available in Europe within a couple of decades after Columbus's voyage. And by the middle of the 16th Century smoking had spread beyond the returning sailors and colonists who had fallen for it on their travels to the New World. Spain and Portugal were clearly the first European countries in which it took off.

The habit then spread to France, probably introduced by Jean Nicot, the French ambassador to Portugal, in 1560. Though some claim that the priest André Thevet was the first to do so in 1556. But it was Nicot who was immortalised by the word nicotine, and *Nicotiana tabacum,* the Latin name for tobacco. It also became known as the Ambassador's herb in France.

As with other imports such as tea and coffee, tobacco was first in vogue as much for its medicinal properties as for pleasure, and its comparative rarity also made it a symbol of wealth. The plant's medicinal virtues included the fact that it reduced tiredness, acted as a painkiller and was used by indigenous Americans to heal wounds. It was also thought to help ease skin infections. Nicot gave it to the French queen Catherine de Medici, who suffered from migraines, and took powdered tobacco as a cure. Thus it was also called the Queen's herb.

SMOKING ON THE RISE

BY THE BEGINNING of the 17th Century, smoking was becoming an increasingly popular activity, and tobacco was already being cultivated by European colonists in the Americas as a commercial crop to be traded with their countries of origin. Major cultivation started in Santo Domingo (1531), in Cuba (1580), and in Brazil (1600). The first plantation in Virginia was established in 1612, and tobacco had become the colony's biggest export within seven years. Maryland followed as an important tobacco producer in 1631. Later, the cultivation of tobacco in North America was to become largely dependent on the use of black slaves, as demand grew on a vast scale.

But the widespread use of tobacco very soon led to two phenomena familiar to smokers today: taxation and demands for it to be banned – both of which would also eventually apply to tea and coffee. Many considered the plant to be evil. In 1586, Philip II of Spain ordered that growers and sellers of tobacco be whipped and threatened with exile, and that the plant 'be publicly burned as a harmful and damaging herb'. Many years earlier, Rodrigo de Jerez, probably the first European to smoke a cigar, had been imprisoned after he was found smoking in Ayamonte, in Andalucia – the smoke coming out of his mouth being seen as evidence of possession by the Devil. By the time he was released, years later, he was understandably pleased to see that many of his countrymen had also become smokers.

In 1624, Pope Urban VIII issued a Bull threatening the citizens of Seville in particular, but smokers in general, with excommunication if they continued to smoke in church: 'feeling no shame, during the celebration of the very holy ordinance of the mass, soiling the sacred vestments with the repugnant humors that tobacco causes, infesting the temples with a repellent odour – to the great scandal of their brethren who keep to the righteous path'. In Persia, Shah Abbas I condemned tobacco users to death; and in 1645, the Czar of Russia ordered smokers to be deported to Siberia, though his successor, Czar Peter the Great (who reigned 1682-1725) was an enthusiastic smoker, by all accounts.

Ignoring its medical uses, the way in which tobacco was consumed for pleasure depended on the fashion current in the various countries in which it was popular. Often, the monarch or court set the example. In Britain (where the first tobacco shops opened before the end of the 17th Century), in France and in Holland, it was smoked in pipes and taken as snuff. In Prussia, in the early years of the 18th Century, the kings Frederick I and Frederick William I led fashion by being keen pipe smokers. Only in Portugal and Spain was tobacco smoked in a form resembling cigars. However, throughout Europe, tobacco remained a habit of the wealthy and those who had visited the New World.

THE WORD 'CIGAR'

*T*HE MOST OBVIOUS origin of the word cigar, is the Mayan term *sik'ar*, meaning smoking – and leading to the Spanish word *cigarro*, which was first recorded in 1730. The Popol Vuh, a Guatemalan Mayan historical text dating from the 16th Century, and translated into Spanish by the priest Fracisco Jimenez in the 18th Century, also mentions the similar words *ciq* or *jiq*. A

much more fanciful theory is that cigar derived from the word *cigaral,* the Spanish word for cicada, the shape of which cigars were supposed to resemble. The Spanish, in any case, came to call their cigars *puros.*

At the beginning of the 17th Century, King Philip III had already decreed that no tobacco grown in the Spanish colonies could be sold to foreigners. In order to control its supply, he later (1614) insisted that all tobacco produced by the colonies should be shipped to Seville. As a result, the city became the centre of the tobacco world.

Cigars using Cuban tobacco were made in Seville from 1676 onwards. A state monopoly (*Estanco*) was announced in 1717, and the royal factories of Seville were founded in 1731. Colonists in Cuba had been growing tobacco from the end of the 16th Century. But there was conflict between the growers (*vegueros*) and big landowners, often absentees living in Spain, as cigars became more popular and demand for high quality tobacco grew. Some of the *vegueros* became tenant farmers, others moved to find new land in areas such as Pinar del Rio (now the source of the world's best cigar tobacco) and Oriente.

The *vegueros* also rebelled against the Spanish monopoly. At this stage no cigars were in fact produced in Cuba, and the Estanco obliged the farmers to sell tobacco – destined for Seville – solely to the government, without being able to control prices. As a result there were uprisings in 1717 and 1721. Another rebellion, in

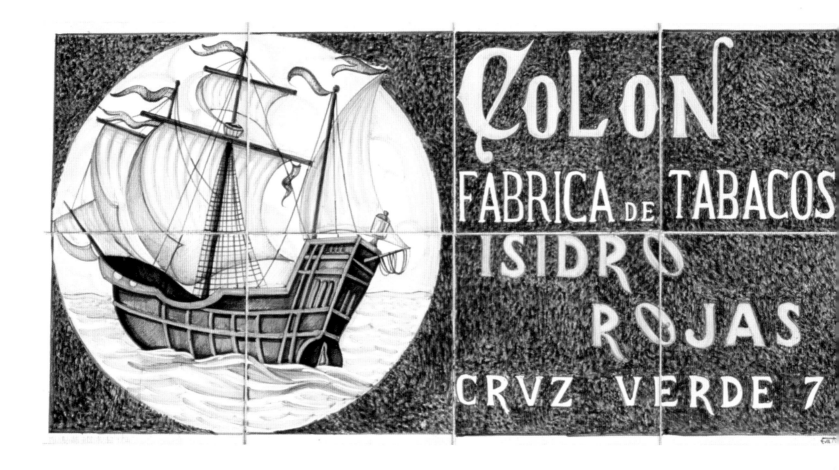

1723, was brutally repressed by the colonial authorities.

The habit of smoking tobacco in cigar form gradually spread to other parts of Europe from Spain during the 18th Century, and by its end, small cigar factories had been set up in Germany, in France (Brittany), and in Liegè (now in Belgium). The word *seegar* (or *segar*) first appeared in English dictionaries in 1735.

North American colonists originally smoked tobacco in pipes – just as native Americans had – though in their case, they were made of clay. Pierre Lorillard set up a factory making tobacco products (later also including cigars) in New York in 1760, but first the cigar probably arrived in North America two years later, when Colonel Israel Putnam, a former officer in the British army, who had taken part in the siege and six-month British occupation of Havana, came home to Connecticut – a colony where tobacco had been grown since the previous century. Putnam, who had also fought in the French and Indian Wars, returned with a supply of both Cuban tobacco and cigars. In due course, cigar factories were set up in the Hartford area and tobacco was grown from Cuban seed. Today, Connecticut Shade wrapper leaves are among the finest produced outside Cuba. The American War of Independence (in the 1770s) was partly prompted as a revolt against tobacco taxes, as well as those on tea (symbolised by the Boston Tea Party); and tobacco actually helped to finance the revolt against British rule by acting as collateral for loans from France.

But cigar smoking didn't really take off in France and Britain until after the Peninsular War of 1808-14, when a

coalition of Spanish, Portuguese and British forces (under the command of the Duke of Wellington) battled Napoleon's armies in the Iberian Peninsula. Both British and French soldiers took home and spread the habit they had acquired while fighting in Spain and Portugal. As a result cigars began to replace pipe smoking and snuff as the fashionable new way to take tobacco in Britain (some 15,000 cigars were imported by the British in 1823, for instance). By then, cigars were also being made in other parts of Europe, particularly in the factories of Holland.

CUBA ON THE MAP

CUBAN GROWERS finally started to make their own cigars on a small scale from the middle of the 18th Century, but the vast majority of cigars were still made in Seville. By that time, the art of cigar making was gradually evolving. The growing of leaf became more sophisticated as the idea of blending leaves, and the use of different types of leaf for the various parts of a cigar was developed. The techniques of curing, fermentation and rolling were also slowly refined, so that the cigars available by the turn of the 19th Century resembled those that we smoke today.

Demand in Europe rose fast in the early years of the 19th Century. But, as demand increased, so did the need for better quality and the Spanish-made *Sevillas*, as they were called, were eventually displaced by cigars made in Cuba

for two reasons: not only were Cuban cigars better made, thanks to the more refined methods of the Cubans; but ready-made cigars survived the sea journey from Cuba very much more successfully than tobacco leaves did. Thus Spanish cigar factories – which had employed more than 5,000 people in 1800 – declined, and the production of Havanas rose rapidly. The process was helped in 1821 by a decree from King Ferdinand VII designed to encourage the manufacture of cigars in Cuba (still a Spanish colony at the time), by relaxing the state monopoly. This easing of the controls on the production and sale of tobacco also had the highly desirable effect of providing a new source of tax revenue for Spain.

The boom in Cuba's cigar industry was dramatic. By the 1850s, there were as many as 9,500 plantations, and hundreds of factories started up in Havana and other Cuban cities. There were almost 1,300 at one stage – though the number had fallen to around 120 by the early 20th Century. Nearly 360 million cigars (the largest number ever) were produced in 1855, compared with 140 million in 1840.

The modern cigar era was now beginning. Branding, for instance, became important: the first Havana trademarks, registered in 1810, being the firms of H. de Cabanas y Carbajal and Bernardino Rencurrel. The first of the great brands still smoked today was Partagas, launched in 1827. Marketing generally also became increasingly important as the industry flourished – leading to innovations such as the cedar cigar box, pioneered by H. Upmann in the 1840s, and the cigar label, pioneered by the Ramon Allones brand (founded in 1837). Later, cigar bands, first introduced by the Dutchman Gustave Bock for his El Aguila de Oro brand, also became an important facet of brand differentiation.

The first major consignment of Cuban cigars arrived in Britain in 1830, stocked by the famous Robert Lewis shop – a tobacconist since 1787, and still a going business. By

Right CRITICS OF SMOKING GOT INTO
THEIR STRIDE AS SOON AS IT BECAME A
CRAZE IN 19TH CENTURY EUROPE. HERE
SMOKERS OF CIGARS AND PIPES ARE
LAMPOONED IN AN ENGLISH PERIODICAL.

Vell Ide sooner have a Pipe of Backer arter a
but oun might as vell be out of the World as ou
of the Fashio

Pub Sep 25 1827 by Tho: McLean Haymarket Lond.

AGE OF PUFFING. PUFF. PUFF. PUFF

1840, sales of Havanas in Britain had climbed to 13 million. But Britain had also started to produce its own *segars* or *seegars*, as they were then called, in 1820. However, Parliament promptly passed a law regulating the industry, and a new import tax ensured that Cuban cigars remained a luxury item, affordable only by the rich. So in Britain, and elsewhere in Europe, both taxation and rising prices due to demand established the image of the Havana cigar as a something associated with wealth. Today, incidentally, the term Havana or Habano is reserved by the Cubans solely for cigars of export quality.

'STOGIE'

CONSUMPTION OF CIGARS in the United States also took off in the early 19th Century. Not only were Cuban cigars being imported, but domestic production also started – with the first American cigar factory founded in Connecticut in 1810, followed by others set up in New York and Pennsylvania. The factory producing the most famous domestic cigars, at Conestoga, Pennsylvania, was to give rise to the name 'stogie', first recorded in 1853. Cultivation of the celebrated Connecticut wrapper leaves began in the 1820s.

Although the Mexican-American War helped to popularise the smoking of cigars in the United States (indeed General Zachary Taylor, commander of the victorious American forces, and later 12th President, was a cigar smoker), they didn't really become a widespread habit until the time of the Civil War (1861-65). By then, the word Havana had become a generic term, and was used for the most expensive American cigars. These 'Clear Havanas' were made with Cuban tobacco and cost five times as much as the normal domestic cigars of the time (most of which used local binders and wrappers combined with a mixture of Cuban and domestic filler leaves).

Following the long tradition of taxing smoking, in 1863 Congress passed a law requiring manufacturers to paste tax stamps on cigar boxes. By the late 19th Century, the cigar had become a status symbol in the United States, as it had in Europe. A tax decrease in the 1870s made cigars even more popular and widely available, and helped to lift domestic production. Today, the United States is easily the world's biggest cigar market.

American presidents have been keen cigar smokers since very early in the history of the United States. Devotees included fourth President James Madison, seventh President Andrew Jackson, and John Quincy Adams, sixth President, who probably first encountered cigars during his time as a diplomat in Holland, France and England. Civil War General (later 18th President) Ulysses S. Grant was often pictured with a cigar in his mouth or hand. More recent American presidents such as John F. Kennedy and Bill Clinton, have also been keen on cigars, in Clinton's case rather controversially.

CIGARS IN LITERATURE

BY THE MID-19th Century, cigars were regularly referred to in literature throughout Europe and the United States. The Briton, Sir Charles Murray, in his book *Visit to Cuba,* published in 1836, was particularly effusive, describing cigars which had been sent back to

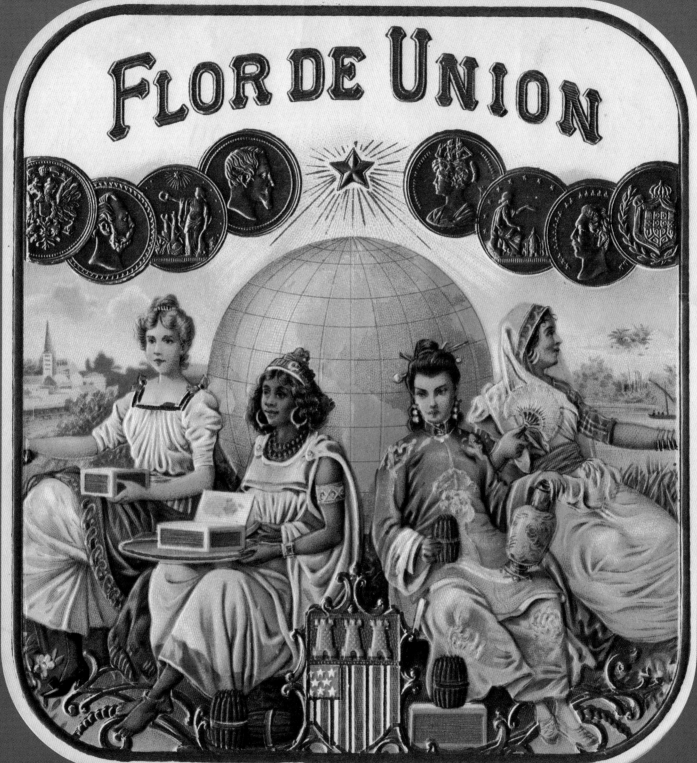

FLOR DE UNION

allowed in the U.S. Congress. And the Victorian poet, critic and politician Edward Bulwer-Lytton (later Lord Lytton) wrote, in 1845, 'A good cigar is as great a comfort to a man as a good cry to a woman'. Lord Byron, actually wrote an ode, *Sublime Tobacco*, in *The Island*.

Many of the greatest British novelists of the Victorian era were not only keen cigar smokers themselves, but wrote about cigars in their work. They included Dickens, Trollope and, above all, perhaps, Thackeray. Thackeray not only wrote about the pleasures of cigar smoking ('one of the greatest creature comforts of my life') but found that cigars helped him to write. There are a number of references to cigars in his great novel – set in the Napoleonic period – *Vanity Fair* (1847). It includes a scene in which his feisty heroine, the adventuress Becky Sharp, briefly smokes after the lumbering, easily manipulated dragoon, Captain Crawley, asks her whether she minds his cigar. He needn't have worried. As Thackeray writes: 'Miss Sharp loved the smell of a cigar out of doors beyond everything in the world'. Becky goes on to marry Crawley later in the novel.

Perhaps the keenest lover of cigars in the whole of American literature was Mark Twain author of *Tom Sawyer* and *Huckleberry Finn*. Twain, who wrote about cigars in his autobiography, and even had a brand named after him, was precocious: he started smoking at the age of eight. When he wrote, he would typically smoke 15 to 20

Havana from England as 'the most delicious cigars that even a meditative philosopher could have dreamed'.

French writers of the19th century frequently mentioned cigars in their work – the novelist Stendhal (author of *The Red and the Black*), for instance. Victor Hugo, the great French novelist, described tobacco as 'the plant that converts thoughts into dreams'. Stephane Mallarme was introduced to cigars by his father – and wrote about his love for them. And the poet and playwright Alfred de Musset took the view that 'Any cigar smoker is a friend, because I know what he feels'.

Among British writers who praised cigars were the historian Thomas Carlyle (1785-1881), who advocated the introduction of cigar smoking to Parliament to calm debate. There was a precedent: cigar smoking was once

cheap cigars a day. In 1871, shortly after getting married, he moved to Hartford, Connecticut, a leading centre of cigar production.

A WAY OF LIFE

CIGARS BECAME SO fashionable amongst European gentlemen that smoking rooms became a feature of houses, clubs and hotels, smoking cars were introduced on trains, and cigar 'divans' opened. Simpson's-in-the-Strand, London's first cigar divan, opened in 1832, and still exists, though as a restaurant.

The fashion even influenced clothing, with the introduction of the smoking jacket, designed to keep clothes free of the lingering smell of cigar smoke. In France, the dinner jacket, or tuxedo, is still called *le smoking*. In Britain, by the late 19th Century, it had become the custom for gentlemen to remain at the table after dinner, smoking cigars with port or brandy, after the ladies had withdrawn to another room. The vogue for cigars was boosted throughout Europe by the fact that leaders and prominent personalities were devotees. In Germany, for instance, Otto von Bismarck (Chancellor 1871-90) was a cigar lover; and in Britain, the fact that the Prince of Wales (the future

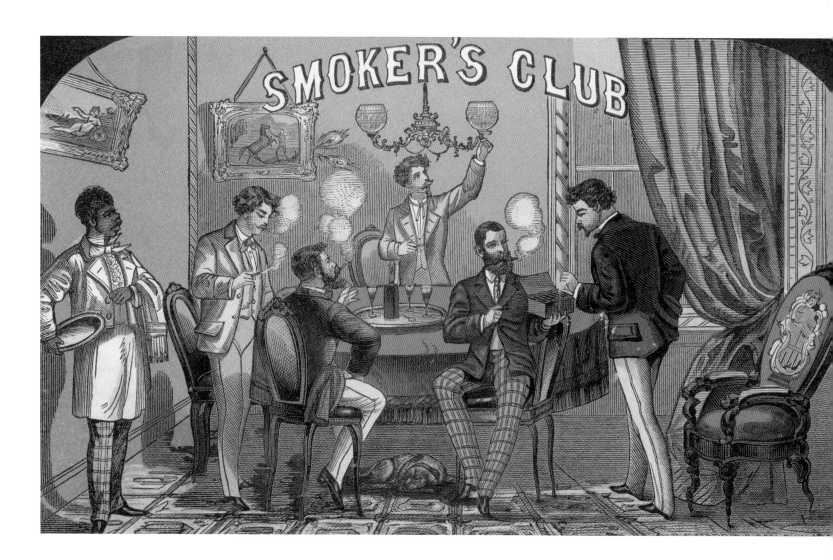

Edward VII) was particularly fond of cigars, also helped to enhance the image of cigars. His mother, Queen Victoria, famously disapproved of the habit, but at the beginning of his nine-year reign in 1901, after an official dinner, he made the famous announcement: 'Gentlemen, you may smoke'. At formal meals in Britain, smoking has traditionally been allowed only at the end, after the Loyal Toast to the monarch. But this convention is now often ignored.

In the United States the sale of cigars peaked in 1907. But sales gradually fell as cigarettes, which were obviously very much cheaper, became the main way of smoking. The 'paper cigar' first appeared when the poor of Seville picked up discarded cigar butts or left-over scraps of tobacco from the factories, shredded them, and then rolled the tobacco in paper. Cigarette smoking had become widespread in Spain, France and Italy by the early 19th Century – and in Greece, Turkey and Russia by the middle of the century. By that time, cigarette factories (the cigarettes were made by hand) had been established. Bizet's opera, *Carmen*, about a girl working in a cigarette factory, was first performed in 1875, based on Prosper Merimee's story of 1845. The habit didn't become popular in Britain and France until after the Crimean War (1853-56), when it was brought back by returning soldiers. But it was the development of cigarette-making machines in the 1880s, and aggressive marketing in Europe and the U.S.A., that led to the decline in cigar smoking.

The rise of cigarettes meant that cigars once again became associated with wealth. During the 1920s, the American poet and columnist F.P. Adams, sneered in *The Rich Man*:

> *The rich man in his motor car,*
> *His country and his town estate.*
> *He smokes a fifty-cent cigar*
> *And jeers at Fate.*

At around the same time, Thomas Marshall, Woodrow Wilson's Vice President, was said to have commented: "What this country really needs is a good five-cent cigar". That ambition wasn't achieved until 30 years later when cigar-making machines allowed cheap cigars to be made.

ON THE SCREEN

CIGARS APPEARED in films from the early silents onwards. In the 1920s, 30s and 40s, their presence partly reflected the fact that they were widely smoked – particularly in America. But they also served a number of symbolic purposes – in much the same way they did in cartoons and caricatures – and do so to this day.

Cigars in Hollywood movies were frequently used either to indicate wealth or, in the case of Charlie Chaplin's films such as *City Lights* and *The Gold Rush* – where the little tramp smokes rich men's discarded cigar ends – poverty, or the memory of wealth. But cigars also provided invaluable props for comedians such as Harold Lloyd, Laurel and Hardy, W.C. Fields and Groucho Marx, often used for visual gags. In pre Second World War Hollywood gangster films, large cigars both represented power (as frequently personified by Edward G. Robinson, himself a keen cigar smoker) and mirrored the real-life popularity of cigars with Mafia bosses such as Al Capone. In westerns, big cigars often symbolised somebody crooked – such as

the unscrupulous railroad boss, the ruthless breaker of Indian treaties, and the card shark. Small or thin cigars, on the other hand, tended to suggest toughness or meanness.

THE CUBAN TRADITION

*I*N CUBA, on the other hand, cigars became a much more important national symbol. This was partly because cigar makers had become key members of the Cuban industrial working class as the 19th Century progressed. Growers, too, were essential to the economy – with tobacco becoming the island's second biggest export product after sugar. In 1864, the factory workers established the unique custom – which continues today – of rollers reading political and literary works, including those of Emile Zola, Victor Hugo, and Alexandre Dumas to their colleagues to entertain and educate them. One of these books was *The Count of Montecristo* – which is why it later became the name of one of Havana's most famous brands. These days, newspapers (admittedly those produced by the government) are read out as well as books, and the radio is also turned on from time to time.

During the 19th Century, the Cubans were in regular conflict with Spain. The colonial power's reluctance to grant them greater autonomy – whilst increasing taxes – gave rise to the first war of independence (1868-78), followed by another war in 1895, during which towns and plantations were torched, and there were many civilian casualties. Given their role in the struggle, tobacco workers in Cuba began to play an important part in national and political life. Cigar production virtually ground to a halt by 1898, and by that time, many cigar workers had emigrated to Florida to escape the conflict and the economic shambles. Many other rollers and growers migrated to the Dominican Republic, Honduras,

Jamaica (where the Temple Hall estates were established in 1876), Mexico and Venezuela.

The United States cigar industry benefited as these émigrés set up cigar factories in towns such as Tampa and Key West. The level of immigration was such that by the beginning of the 20th Century, 12,000 of the 18,000 workers in Key West were Cubans, mostly working in the cigar industry.

Just as today Floridians of Cuban origin are amongst the most implacable enemies of the communist regime, these 19th Century Cubans émigrés helped to fund the the final uprising against Spain, led by the Cuban national hero Jose Marti in 1895. There can be no more pointed symbolism than the fact that even Marti's order for the revolt was sent from Key West to Cuba hidden in a cigar.

Cuba fell under first the direct, and then the indirect, control of the United States during the early 20th Century, and an economic recovery began. At one stage, the Tobacco Trust imported no fewer than 291 cigar brands into the United States, allowing the Cubans to export some 250 million cigars a year. The Trust was set up by the notorious tobacco magnate 'Buck' Duke, and controlled 90 per cent of Havana cigar exports by 1902. Foreign involvement in Cuba's cigar industry had, until then, been confined to the Spanish and, to a lesser extent, the British and Germans. It was acknowledged, however, that cigars made by independent producers, the *'Independientes'* were better than those of the companies owned by the Trust – so that by 1905, the Trust's share of exports had fallen to 52 per cent. Labour relations were also poor in the Trust's factories, and in 1932, production of most its biggest brands, such as La Corona and Henry Clay, was moved to Trenton, New Jersey.

Innovations, such as the machine production of cigars, were attempted in the 1920s, led in Cuba by Por Larranaga – in the face of great initial opposition from the firm's

Opposite THE TOBACCO MAGNATE JAMES 'BUCK' DUKE'S NOTERIETY WAS CAUSED IN LARGE PART BY HIS ATTEMPTS TO MODERNISE AND STREAMLINE THE INDUSTRY.

rollers. They were abandoned in 1936, not to return until the late 1940s. Developments were also taking place in Cuban leaf production during this turbulent period. A new, disease-resistant variety of *Tabaco Negro Cubano* (Cuban cigar tobacco) called Habanenis was produced in 1907, followed by the Criollo variety in 1941 – today the basis for all Havana cigars.

Machine production in the United States also started, with the result that machine-made cigars rose from 10 per cent of total U.S. cigar production in 1924, to a huge 98 per cent by the 1950s.

The status of cigar workers meant that they continued to be in the vanguard of political awareness after Fidel Castro's revolution against the dictator General Fulgencio Batista in 1959. Many workers in the tobacco industry were descendants of former African slaves, and they had hitherto, like most Cubans of African extraction, been excluded from political power. As with Jose Marti, the cigar was a symbol of Castro's revolution. *El Commandante* was particularly fond of cigars: when he was a prisoner he was sent messages hidden in them. Ironically, he gave up smoking over a decade ago – theoretically, at least, to set a healthy example to fellow Cubans.

There was also a revolution in Cuban cigar factories themselves – with women starting to roll cigars in the early 1960s. Until then, only men had performed this task and women were confined to selecting leaves – sometimes sorting them on their thighs, and thus giving rise to the famous myth about cigars being rolled on the thighs of Cuban maidens.

THE CUBAN REVOLUTION

CASTRO WASN'T, at first, a Communist, but he was a socialist, and he started to nationalise Cuban and foreign assets when he came to power. The cigar industry – much of which was American owned before Castro – was nationalised along with everything else, and came under the control of the state monopoly, Cubatabaco. Pre-revolutionary cigars have since become collectors' items.

The United States reacted by imposing an embargo on Cuba in 1962 – which is still in action at the time of writing, more than 40 years later. The embargo meant that

Havana cigars could no longer be legally imported into the U.S., apart from in small quantities for personal use. This was a substantial blow to Cuba's cigar industry, even though the number of Havanas exported to the United States had fallen to only 44 million a couple of years before Castro's revolution.

As a result of nationalisation, and the later move to Communism, a number of Cuba's leading cigar factory owners such as the Cifuentes, Menendez and Palicio families departed the island, determined to set up their businesses in places such as Florida, the Dominican Republic, Honduras, Mexico and the Canary Islands. They did so successfully, often using the names of the Havana brands they had owned before the revolution. That is why cigars called Partagas, Romeo Y Julieta, and H.Upmann are made in the Dominican Republic, and Punch and Hoyo de Monterrey come from Honduras – often with bands and box labels almost identical to their Cuban namesakes. But, though they are frequently very good cigars, these brands bear no similarity, in terms of flavour or aroma, to their Havana counterparts – other than in name and packaging.

The former Cuban factory owners, and their inheritors, also started to make extremely satisfactory new brands, often in association with the major American cigar companies – so that today, the Dominican Republic produces many of the world's finest cigars (some of them able to give the Cubans a run for their money), and over half of the cigars imported by the United States. Honduras has also become a major player in the cigar world, particularly in the United States market. Non-Cuban hand-made cigars are also a major feature of the German market, for instance.

Many felt that the quality of Cuban cigars deteriorated immediately after the revolution – something the Cubans understandably denied. But the criticism was partially valid: some of Cuba's best cigar makers had, after all,

emigrated, and the economic factors (including the American embargo) put pressure on the Cubans to cut production costs. In answer to the critics, however, they created the Cohiba brand in 1968 – designed, at the time, to be the best in the world.

Cigars, of course, have always been something of a capitalist symbol in the public imagination, associated with the wealthy and powerful. At one stage the communist Cubans found this irony surrounding their most prestigious export embarrassing. There was even a time, soon after the revolution, when some in the hierarchy were determined to abolish brands and create just one 'People's Cigar'. But, luckily for the rest of us, financial necessity meant that wiser thinking prevailed, and the cigar industry attained a new importance – as an obvious way of accumulating much needed foreign exchange.

At the time of the revolution, there were some 1,000 different types of Havana cigar (brands and sizes), and the Cubans realized they had to streamline and rationlise the cigar industry. In 1979, for instance, they standardised sizes and reduced the number of brands they produced, cutting out oddities such as the famous Larranaga Magnum. Another rationalisation took place in 1993. As a result, all Cuban cigar factories today produce more than one brand, though some specialize in particular sizes, and others in specific blends and flavours. Some critics argue that standards fell as a result of these changes, but since the early

1990s the Cubans have realized that quality is the only serious advantage their cigars have over rivals from the Dominican Republic and Honduras, and they have made strenuous efforts to keep standards high and consistent to justify their prices. As a result, by the end of the 1990s, the Cubans actually launched a number of new brands, such as Vegas Robaina, San Cristobal and Cuaba, and increased tobacco acreage to cope with the rapidly rising demand for hand-made cigars. By the end of the 90s, Cuba was exporting around 120 million hand-made cigars a year, compared with only 30 million just after the revolution. There was one blot, however: in 1990, the legendary Davidoff brand, synonymous the world over with cigars, moved production to the Dominican Republic after a dispute with the Cuban government. At the time of writing, there are 33 Havana brands (including machine-made) available for export.

There have been a series of trademark disputes, over the last few years, between the Cubans and manufacturers in the Dominican Republic and elsewhere using the same brand names – including legendary marques such as

Above and opposite GERMANY AND SWITZERLAND *(ALSO*
THE NETHERLANDS) *HAVE LONG HAD THEIR OWN CIGAR*
INDUSTRIES, TYPICALLY USING IMPORTED LEAF,
ESPECIALLY FROM JAVA *AND* SUMATRA.

PATRON

MARQUE DÉPOSÉE

Above THE MACANUDO FUMOIR IN CLARIDGES HOTEL,
IN LONDON, IS A PRESTIGIOUS CIGAR BAR.

Cohiba and Montecristo. And, if the United States embargo is finally lifted, we can be confident that the people to benefit the most will be the lawyers – as the Cubans fight the other trademark owners in the courts.

THE GREAT CIGAR BOOM

*T*HESE LEGAL STRUGGLES are partly a result of the cigar boom of the 1990s. The boom, which became apparent in 1993, can partly be ascribed to the launch of the magazine *Cigar Aficianado* in September of the previous year and the appearance of books such as my best-selling *The Cigar Companion* (1993) – which sold around 400,000 copies in hardback worldwide. These sorts of publications led to an increased awareness and knowledge of hand made cigars. There were obviously other reasons as well. Of course cigars are safer than cigarettes, and it is possible that many former cigarette smokers switched. But more convincing is the fact that the economies of counties such as the United States, France, the United Kingdom, and Germany were all either growing or recovering from recession by the mid-1990s – meaning that more disposable income could be spent on luxuries such as cigars. This was particularly true for those working in sectors such as finance, property and the law, many of whom saw their incomes soar as a result of the 1980s boom in some of these countries. They were able to spend freely on status symbols without fear of embarrassment. This is certainly true in the United States (and countries, such as Britain, where the economic cycle is strongly linked to that of the U.S.). The figures speak for themselves: the Dow Jones index rose from 780 in August 1982 to reach over 11,000 by early 2000 (it fell to 8,000 by 2003). The combination of these reasons added to vigorous marketing resulted in premium cigar sales rocketing, with an estimated 100,000 or more new cigar smokers in the United States in 1994. Imports of premium cigars to the United States rose from 107 million in 1993, to 297 million in 1996, and up to a staggering 500 million by 1997. An indication of the fact that premium cigars had actually become fashionable was that the age profile of cigar smokers became significantly lower during the 1990s – with the fastest growing segment of the hand-made cigar market in the United States in 1993-4 being 26 to 38 year olds. Premium cigar sales also rose significantly in Europe, and in the wealthier nations of South East Asia.

The fact that cigars became fashionable also had many collateral effects, such as the growth of cigar dinners, cigar auctions and cigar-orientated or cigar-friendly restaurants and bars.

Hotels also got in on the act: in London, Claridge's opened its Macanudo Fumoir in 2002, and many other leading hotels around the world have bars specializing in top-quality cigars, which are now properly stored thanks to much improved staff training.

Following *Cigar Aficianado's* lead, a number of new cigar magazines flourished around the world – in Spain, Austria, and France (*Amateur de Cigare*), as well as in the United States – and shelves full of new books have been published, when once there was only a handful.

There are also regular features about cigars in newspapers and general interest magazines; and TV films reported on the boom. The internet also had its part to play: by the late 1990s, dozens of cigar-related web sites had blossomed, as well as on-line cigar magazines. Even the horse, owned by Allen Paulson, that dominated the American 1995 and 1996 racing seasons was a colt called Cigar. But a less welcome consequence of this burgeoning of cigar culture is the major increase in the number of fake Havanas (and, increasingly, premium brands made in the Dominican

Republic) which have appeared around the world.

WOMEN AND CIGARS

ANOTHER, MUCH-HYPED, side-effect of cigar chic is that many women started to smoke premium cigars. The trend was led by supermodels and films stars such as Claudia Schiffer, Linda Evangelista, Sharon Stone, Whoopi Goldberg, Drew Barrymore and Demi Moore – many of whom have been featured on the covers of magazines such as *Cigar Aficionado* and *Smoke*, as well as being pictured with stogies in their mouths.

Women have smoked cigars in Cuba, South and Central America, and Spain ever since modern cigars were first manufactured, though never to the same extent as men. They have also done so in other countries since the 19th Century. Most famously, 1930s Berlin had a number of women-only cigar clubs. But until recently, European women (such as George Sand, Colette, Marlene Dietrich and Virginia Woolf) who smoked cigars were seen as either making a point about their sexuality or challenging the male establishment. Indeed, cigar smoking was regarded as an almost exclusively male activity, thought to be positively unpleasant for women. 'I do not believe that there was ever an Aunt Tabithy who could abide cigars,' wrote Donald G. Mitchell in his *Reveries of a Bachelor* in 1850. In the same vein, C.B. Hartley, in *The Gentleman's Book of Etiquette* (1873), advised: 'Do not smoke in the street until after dark, and then remove your cigar from your mouth if you meet a lady'.

So just why have large numbers of women started smoking cigars over the last few years? It could, of course, be just a matter of jumping on the bandwagon, with cigars being nothing more than the latest fashion accessory. Or perhaps women now smoke cigars for the same reason

Above HAVANA GIRL DEMONSTRATES THAT ELEGANCE CAN BE A LARGE CIGAR.

many men have smoked them for the past 150 years: to assert power, wealth and prestige – as symbolised by the poster for the film *The First Wives Club,* where Goldie Hawn, Bette Midler and Diane Keaton were pictured with fat cigars, celebrating victory over their husbands.

But the trend seems to be a genuine one and more women – mostly highly-paid professionals – are certainly smoking cigars today than in the past. In America, it is thought that more than 200,000 cigars a year are sold to women. And women-only cigar clubs and events are now common. In 1998, *Cigar Aficionado* ran a feature about eight women who had broken into the previously very male world of cigar retailing. And in 1999, Jean Clarke, manager of the cigar department of Harrods department store, in London, was nominated as one of the world's top five Havana retailers by the Cubans.

The rise of non-Havana

The cigar boom also benefited a number of producer-countries other than Cuba, the Dominica Republic and Honduras. Increased investment meant that Costa Rica became a source of good leaf, and Ecuador began to produce decent wrapper tobacco. Countries such Brazil, Mexico, and Nicaragua all have old cigar making traditions, but now their leaf is also in demand from manufacturers elsewhere: Mexican binder tobacco, for instance, is now widely used by a number of leading premium brands. Cameroon in West Africa produces some of the finest dark wrapper leaves in the world, and the Indonesian islands of Java and Sumatra, which have old links with the cigar industries of Holland, Switzerland and Germany (for machine-mades in recent times) are now also important as suppliers of wrapper leaf to New World producers. And the Philippines and the Canary Islands, historically linked to Spain, produce leaf used by a number of manufacturers, as well as making their own cigars.

Around the middle of 1997 there were signs that the cigar boom was levelling out, and by 2000, there were an estimated 100 million unsold hand-made cigars in the United States. One of the reasons for this glut was the appearance on the market of what became contemptuously known in the industry as 'Don Nobodies' – cheap hand-mades, not properly matured, which suddenly appeared to meet demand created by new smokers. Another reason is that, as a result of shortages in the mid-90s (larger sizes were particularly difficult to find), many enthusiastic smokers started stocking up heavily when production, particularly in the Domincan Republic, was eventually increased. Those stocks took some time to be smoked. As a result prices at the bottom end of the handmade market fell (the 'Don Nobodies' also undercut the prices of established brands).

The end of the 20th Century, and the beginning of the 21st, saw major changes in the ownership of some of the world's most important cigar producers. Altadis SA, formed after a merger of the former Spanish and French tobacco monopolies, Tabacalera and SEITA (Tabacalera actually took over SEITA) became the world's biggest cigar company in 1999 – partly because SEITA had taken over Consolidated Cigar (America's biggest cigar business) during the same year. In a surprise move, the company, which now has around 25 per cent of the world's cigar sales, also acquired 50 per cent of Habanos SA, the state-owned Cuban export monopoly. Habanos was set up in 1994, and technically owns all Cuban brands outside the United States, as well as co-owning a number of Casa del Habano shops around the world.

After the shakeout at the end of the 1990s, the cigar market started to grow again in the U.S.A. and elsewhere in 2002 and 2003 – in line with economic improvement. At the time of writing, hand-made cigar sales in the United States, which represents 65 per cent of the world market, are between 250-300 million annually. There is one important change, however: today's market for cigars is about as knowledgeable as it has ever been. This means that cigar manufacturers are now launching new sizes of famous brands (the Cubans unveiled three new sizes of the formerly rare Trinidad late in 2003), and specialized cigars firmly aimed at connoisseurs – such as 'vintage' cigars, and 'limited editions' of various Havana brands. Fewer cigars are being sold today than at the height of the boom – but to people who appreciate them more.

Making CIGARS

Left ALL AGES WORK OVERTIME DURING

HARVEST IN THE TOBACCO FIELDS

OF CUBA.

MAKING FINE CIGARS is something like making wine: the quality of the grapes, the climatic conditions, the soil, and the care taken over blending, fermentation and bottling are crucial to the quality of the product.

*L*IKE WINE, cigars are natural products, which continue to change the longer they are kept: they will improve or deteriorate according to how well they are handled and stored. Unlike wine, the world's leading cigar brands are produced and made almost one hundred per cent by hand. It is an astonishingly laborious process.

The transition from tobacco seed to the cigar you smoke is particularly complex. It is composed of dozens of stages, each one of which must be strictly controlled and monitored to achieve the highest quality. The difference between good and bad cigars is totally determined by how good the tobacco is, by the growing conditions, and by how carefully it is matured. The skill of the roller is also paramount. Virtually every labour-intensive stage of tobacco growing and cigar manufacture contributes to the quality and eventually to the price of a premium cigar - meaning an expensive hand-made cigar.

Hand-made cigars consist of three parts: the filler, binder, and the wrapper. Each of these parts has a different role in a cigar, and each makes a contribution to its flavour, and to how much you enjoy it. Leaves destined for different parts of a cigar are grown and matured in subtly different ways, and chosen for specific purposes in the finished product.

Tobacco leaves first have to be cured in order to help preserve them, to remove impurities, and to make them sufficiently flexible for rolling. Fermentation and maturation are additional purification processes which help to develop the flavour of the leaves before they are finally rolled. For more details, see page 47.

What follows is a description of how the best Havana cigars are made. The technical terms used are, unless otherwise stated, specific to Cuban cigars. However, the world's other premium cigar producers use essentially similar methods, based on the Cuban model.

GROWING AND HARVESTING

*T*OBACCO SEEDS must be planted in well-drained, level fields, to avoid being washed away. After planting, a thin covering of straw or cloth is traditionally used to protect them from the sun and the wind. This is removed as they start germinating. They have to be planted in very loose soil – broken up by ploughs harnessed to animals, rather than tractors – so that the soil is not compacted. They are carefully irrigated from below. This is not organic farming: pesticides are used to protect the vulnerable seedlings from parasites. These days, some seeds are grown in polystyrene containers, protected by plastic tunnels.

The best Havana cigar tobacco is raised in the red soil of the Pinar del Rio area of Cuba, where the growing season is from November to February. This is the island's dry season (*La Seca*). Before it comes the wet season (middle of May to early October), during which heavy rain ensures that the soil is well irrigated. During *La Seca*, conditions are perfect for growing tobacco: with eight hours a day of sunshine, average temperature highs of 26-27 C (80 F), and average humidity of 64 per cent. Humidity is a key factor in the production of top-quality leaf, as it is later in storing cigars.

In the fields (*vegas*) the plants are spaced around 0.6 m (2ft) apart, in rows which are about 1 m (3 ft) apart. As they grow, flower buds appear, and have to be removed by hand in order to ensure the growth of large leaves. This process leads to the growth of side shoots, which the farmer (*veguero*) has to remove by hand. Cigar tobacco plants can produce 16-20 leaves each in the best conditions.

Wrapper leaves, from the variety of tobacco called *corojo*, are grown in a distinctively different way from those destined for other parts of the cigar. Some ten to 20 days after the seedlings are transplanted, farmers on stilts erect a canopy of muslin sheets, held up by high wooden poles, over the fields. Since the wrapper is the part of the cigar that gives it its appearance, wrapper leaves must be unblemished, thin and elastic, to facilitate rolling. This covering technique (called *tapado*) helps to prevent the leaves becoming too oily or coarse, as they would do in direct sunlight, and produces larger leaves. A single *corojo* plant can wrap up to 32 cigars. Growth of wrapper tobacco takes up to 90 days, depending on the weather.

Right TOBACCO LEAVES
FRESH FROM HARVESTING.

The best cigar wrapper leaves are grown on sandy and sandy-loam soil with a high moisture content.

The wrapper (*capa*) is the most expensive part of a cigar, and growing conditions have to be virtually ideal, which explains why top-quality wrapper leaves come from very few sources. The finest still come from the Vuelta Abajo area of Cuba. Good non-Cuban wrappers are grown in Cameroon, Connecticut, Ecuador, Sumatra, Honduras, Mexico, Nicaragua and Costa Rica. The Dominican Republic, despite its large cigar industry, and proximity to Cuba, doesn't generally have suitable growing conditions for good wrapper tobacco, but the last decade has seen some notable and successful attempts to produce high quality wrappers, particularly by the Fuente family.

America's famous Connecticut Shade wrapper leaves were first grown more than 100 years ago from imported Cuban seed. They are produced, in the area north of Hartford, in 3 m (10 ft) high cheesecloth tents in which the temperature

Growing tobacco

RIGHT: PREPARING THE SOIL FOR SEED. *A SQUARE METRE CAN PRODUCE 90 TO 150 SEEDLINGS. AFTER 45 DAYS (WHICH IN CUBA COINCIDES WITH THE SECOND HALF OF OCTOBER), THE SEEDLINGS ARE READY TO BE PLANTED OUT.*

BELOW: *ABOUT 18-20 DAYS AFTER THE SEEDLINGS ARE PLANTED OUT, THE SOIL AT THE BASE OF THE PLANTS IS BANKED UP IN ORDER TO PROMOTE DEVELOPMENT OF STRONG ROOTS - JUST AS WITH OTHER CROPS.*

BELOW: *WRAPPER LEAVES ARE GROWN IN SPECIAL CONDITIONS, UNDER A CANOPY OF MUSLIN SHEETS. EACH PLANT IS INDIVIDUALLY ATTACHED TO THE FRAME BY STRINGS AND CAREFULLY IRRIGATED.*

and humidity are carefully controlled and the plants are protected from the sun, just like their Cuban counterparts. The cultivation of Connecticut Shade is possibly the most expensive and labour-intensive of all forms of American agriculture, costing around $30,000 per 5000 m (one acre) to produce and process.

Sun-grown leaves, used for the filler and binder (the variety called *criollo* in Cuba) are best grown on silt-loam and clay-loam soils, and take between 45 and 70 days to become ready for harvesting. Just where the leaves are on the stem makes a difference to their flavour and how they will be used. Those from sun-grown plants are classified in six categories, depending on where they are (those on wrapper plants have nine categories).

The leaves are also classified by colour and texture: into *ligero* (light), from the top of the plant; *volado* from the bottom; *seco* (dry), from the middle of the plant; and *medio tiempo* (half or average texture). There are similar classifications for wrapper leaves: *viso* (glossy); *seco*,

Above SUN-GROWN LEAVES ON A DOMINICAN REPUBLIC PLANTATION. THE SUNLIGHT BRINGS OUT A RICH VARIETY OF FLAVOURS IN THESE PLANTS, WHICH WILL BE USED AS FILLER LEAVES AND BINDERS.

amarillo (yellow); *medio tiempo* and *quebrado* (broken).

As a rule, the longer tobacco leaves are exposed to the sun (and depending, obviously, on the strength of the sunlight), the oilier and higher in sugar content they will be. This means that the leaves at the top of a tobacco plant are normally the strongest in flavour.

For this reason, *ligero* leaves have a full flavour and burn slowly. *Seco* leaves are medium flavoured, slow burning, and are used as filler. They also contribute most to the aroma of a cigar. *Volado* leaves (the word means 'flown away') burn well, and are used for binders, and milder fillers. Because of the *tapado* technique, wrapper leaves usually have little flavour. Leaves are also graded by size and physical condition – with broken or unhealthy leaves ending up in cigarettes, machine-made cigars, or those not suitable for export.

You need only know that (in Cuba, anyway) each plant has to be visited up to 170 times by the *vegueros* in just four months, to realize just how very labour-intensive it is to grow the best tobacco.

Harvesting begins, at the earliest, about 40 days after planting out, and takes place from the beginning of December to early March. Each leaf has to be picked by hand, and only two or three can be taken from a plant at one time, so that other leaves can continue to grow. As a result, a single sun-grown plant can take almost a month to harvest completely – usually in six phases. This also adds to the expense of producing the finest cigars.

When they are harvested, leaves – which are allowed to wilt slightly to reduce the danger of breakage – are removed one by one, using a single movement of the hand. Harvesting starts at the base of the plant, but leaves from the very bottom (*mananita*) are too small to be used for Havanas, and end up in machine-mades. Shade-grown plants are taller and have more leaves, so they are picked in as many as nine phases, each taking around a week, again starting from the base. These are called: *mananita* (little tomorrow), *libre de pie* (literally, free of foot), *uno y medio* (one and a half), *primer centro ligero* (first light centre), *segundo centro ligero* (second light centre), *primer centro fino* (first thin centre), *segundo centro fino* (second thin centre), *centro gordo* (thick centre) and *corona* (crown). The finest leaves are found in the middle of the plant. *Corona* leaves are usually too oily to be used for wrappers, except for domestic consumption, and are normally used as filler leaves. *Libre de pie* leaves and *mananitas* are also rejected as wrappers. After being removed, the leaves are sorted into small bundles, according to their type.

Leaf production from transplantation to the end of the harvest takes around 120 days.

Some non-Cuban cigar manufacturers such as General Cigar (for their Macanudo brand) and Dunhill have occasionally declared 'vintages' – which refer to the year of harvest, not manufacture.

CURING AND FERMENTATION

AFTER SORTING, leaves are taken for curing to traditional tobacco barns. See page 00. In the barn needle and thread are used to sew the leaves into pairs, after which they are hung on poles (*cujes*) placed on racks. The poles, carrying fifty pairs of leaves each, are raised horizontally on the racks, and are lifted progressively higher in the barn as curing continues, in order to allow air to circulate around them. This method of air curing is very much shorter than the flue (or heat) curing methods used for cigarette tobacco. Once curing is complete, the different types of leaves are tied in large bundles (*gavillas*), once more according to their type.

Until the mid-1990s, Cuban wrapper leaves were cured in the traditional barns, but since then, these highly-prized leaves have been cured in units with sophisticated temperature and humidity controls to create optimum conditions around the clock. As a result of this investment, they are now cured much faster – in only 25 days.

The *gavillas* are now sent to the sorting house (*escogida*), where they first have to be fermented, done by arranging them in stacks about 1 m (3 ft) high, covered by jute cloth. The process is rather like composting, and is helped by the moisture still present in the leaves. Fermentation produces heat, but constant supervision ensures that none of piles becomes hotter than 33 C (92 F). Leaves from higher up in the tobacco plant need to be fermented for longer, because they are not only thicker, but contain more oil. Wrapper leaves take 30 days or more to ferment; and sun-grown leaves (*ligero)* from the top of the plant also take about the same time. *Seco* and *volado* leaves from lower down are fermented for only 25 days. Once this first fermentation is complete, the jute is removed, and the piles are broken up so that the leaves can cool down.

Now the leaves must be graded. They are first shaken to separate them, then dampened with water, and aired. Wrapper leaves are sorted into as many as 50 different types, according to colour, size, quality, and texture. Leaves which don't make the grade are used for other purposes. Sun-grown leaves are sorted into three sizes and the three categories (*ligero, volado and seco*) of flavour (*tiempos*) essential for blending fillers, and making binders. Again, rejected leaf ends up in non-export cigars and cigarettes.

At this stage, wrapper leaves, which only need one fermentation, are packed into square bales (*tercios*) made from palm bark and sent to warehouses to be aged. So-called 'green' cigars, once popular in the United States, have wrapper leaves which are picked early. As they are not matured, the wrappers have little flavour or aroma.

It's a different story for filler and binder leaves, which now have to go to the stripping house (*despalillo*). First they have to be moistened (*moja*) with a mixture of water and tobacco juice to make them pliable. The job of stripping has traditionally been performed by women,

often on a wooden board resting on their legs, or piles of leaves on their laps. It is this that gave rise to the provocative and long-standing myth of cigars being rolled on the thighs of Cuban maidens.

During the stripping process, filler leaves have part of their central veins removed. They are also graded once again into the three *tiempos*, and unsuitable leaves are rejected. The all-important wrapper leaves are stripped later, in the cigar factories themselves, moistened by water alone.

After grading, the leaves are flattened by being tied in bunches of 50, and pressed between boards. This is followed by a second fermentation, during which, the leaves are again arranged in large piles (*burros*) – sometimes as much as 2 m (6 ft) tall, covered with hessian. Their fermentation is helped by the earlier moistening (*moja*). As before, the thicker, fuller flavoured leaves from the top of the plant need the longest fermentation. It lasts for 90 days for *ligero* leaves, 60 days for *seco,* and 45 days for *volado.* This second fermentation is much more powerful than the first. Thermometers are inserted into the burros, and if the temperature reaches 42–43 C (110–112 F), the pile is broken up, the leaves allowed to cool, and then 'turned': re-stacked the other way round to make sure that fermentation takes place evenly. This re-stacking might well happen several times for each pile.

After the lengthy period of curing, grading and fermentation, the tobacco is aired on racks for a few days. Then it is finally ready to be sent to the warehouse or factory, packed in hessian bales called *pacas.*

Once there, the leaves go through one last process in order to get them into perfect condition, and to give them peak flavour, before manufacture. This is ageing. The strong *ligero* leaves are aged for at least two years; *seco* leaves need 12-18 months, and *volado* leaves are aged for at least nine months.

The wrapper leaves which arrived earlier in their *tercios* are

Curing and fermentation

ABOVE: *FERMENTATION, WHOSE MAIN AIM IS TO SWEAT OUT IMPURITIES, INCLUDING NITROGEN COMPOUNDS, WHICH IS WHY THERE IS A VERY STRONG SMELL OF AMMONIA IN THE SORTING HOUSE DURING THIS PROCESS. LEVELS OF TAR AND ACIDITY ARE ALSO REDUCED, AND THE AMOUNT OF NICOTINE IN THE LEAVES CAN FALL BY AS MUCH AS 50 PER CENT. SUCCESSFUL FERMENTATION IS ESSENTIAL TO HOW A CIGAR EVENTUALLY TASTES AND SMELLS, AND IT ALSO HELPS THE VARIOUS TYPES OF LEAVES TO ATTAIN A UNIFORM COLOUR AND TEXTURE.*

ABOVE: *TOBACCO LEAVES CURING IN A TRADITIONAL TOBACCO BARN (CASA DE TABACO) ON THE PLANTATION. HERE THEY ARE LEFT TO, CHANGE COLOUR AND DRY FOR BETWEEN 45 AND 60 DAYS, DEPENDING ON THE WEATHER. THE BARNS HAVE LARGE DOORS AT EACH END, AND FACE WEST SO THAT THE SUN HEATS ONE END IN THE MORNING, AND THE OTHER IN THE LATE AFTERNOON. TEMPERATURE, LIGHT AND HUMIDITY ARE CAREFULLY CONTROLLED, PARTLY BY OPENING AND CLOSING THE BARN DOORS AS NECESSARY. DURING THIS PROCESS, THE LEAVES GO FROM GREEN TO A GOLDEN BROWN COLOUR, AS THEY OXIDISE, AND AS CHLOROPHYLL GIVES WAY TO BROWN CAROTENE.*

aged for a minimum of six months. The palm bark they are wrapped in helps the leaves to stay at a constant humidity.

The Connecticut Shade wrapper leaves produced by General Cigar are aged twice. After they have been harvested in Connecticut, they are sent, by ship, to the Dominican Republic, where they are fermented. In early autumn, the leaves are baled and returned to the cool of Connecticut for what is called their 'winter sweat,' an ageing process of seven months. Then, in spring, they are shipped back to the Dominican Republic, where they are aged for at least another year.

For some of the top Cuban brands, such as Cohiba, the *ligero* and *seco* leaves are selected once more, and fermented a third time in barrels in the cigar factory. This gives Cohiba in particular its distinctive, strong taste that is esteemed by many smokers of the brand.

Careful curing is crucial to the flexibility of tobacco leaf when it is rolled, and the lengthy fermentation and maturing process is essential to produce the required flavour and aroma of the cigar leaves, as well as the removal of impurities. Because of the fermentation process, cigar tobacco is much lower in tar, nicotine and acidity than cigarette tobacco.

If you can smell a vague odour of ammonia coming from a cigar, you can be sure the leaves haven't been properly matured. As a rule, the longer leaves are fermented and matured, the finer the flavour.

IN THE FACTORY

THERE ARE ONLY a handful of factories (*fabricas*) in Havana today producing hand-made cigars, when once there were dozens. However, several new factories have been built in Cuba since the 1990s boom. The latest is the new H.Upmann factory, which opened only recently in the Havana suburb of Vedado. Factory names were all changed at the time of the revolution to ones which were considered ideologically sound, but they are still often referred to by their pre-Revolutionary names, and still have their old brand signs outside. Thus the Partgas factory became Franscisco Perez German, Romeo y Julieta became Briones Montoto, La Corona became Fernando Roig, and the original H. Upmann factory became the Jose Marti factory. The factories each make several brands, but usually ones of similar type or flavour. Some factories also specialize in making particular sizes. At the Partagas factory in downtown Havana, for instance, the emphasis is on full-bodied cigars. These include Partagas, of course, but also Bolivar and Ramon Allones.

The cigar factory is where all the work and dedication to quality and careful selection put into the growing and maturing of cigar tobacco finally falls into place to produce the cigars we smoke. Here the key factors are not only the skill of the rollers, but the vigilance of factory managers in ensuring that only cigars which are up to scratch – and true to their brand – are eventually exported.

By the time they leave the factory, the leaves of hand-made Havana cigars will have been through around 200 different stages from the day the seed was planted. And it will have been more than three years since the oldest leaves were picked.

Wrapper leaves, as you might expect, receive particular attention. Once they arrive at the factory in their *tercios*, they have to be taken out and shaken loose from each other. By now, they are fairly brittle and have to be moistened (by workers called *zafadores*), so that they can be stripped, and sorted once more. First the tips of the leaves are dipped in water, and then the leaves (in bunches of 40-50) are held under a fine spray of water. Excess droplets are removed, to avoid staining, by a further shaking. Finally, the leaves are left in bunches on racks for about 24 hours with the humidity controlled at 95 per cent. This process gives the leaves – some of them almost translucent by now – a smooth, almost silky texture.

After stripping the wrapper leaves (see page 52), the women then grade the leaves once more by size and colour, stretching and flattening them as they do so. Wrapper leaves are graded in up to 20 different shades and sizes. They are later gathered in bunches of 25, according to the size (*vitola*) of cigar they will eventually adorn. Each wrapper leaf should be big enough for two cigars.

Filler and binder leaves are removed from their bales, and carefully examined. Those which are still too moist are aired on racks. Then they are stored in wooden barrels until it is time to use them. Next comes blending (see page 52).

Brands obviously have to have a consistent and distinctive flavour, which means that the blend must always be the same from year to year. The harvest in any one year might not always allow this, so big stocks of matured leaf from earlier harvests have to be on hand to ensure consistency. This stockpiling adds to the cost of the finest cigars.

The ratio of different leaves in the filler determines the flavour and aroma of each brand. Full-bodied cigars, such as Partagas, have a higher proportion of *ligero;* whilst milder cigars (Hoyo de Monterrey, for instance) have a greater percentage of *volado* and *seco* leaves. The very full flavour of Cuban Bolivars actually comes from a blend in which there is more *seco* than *volado*, rather than reflecting a particularly

Opposite TOOLS OF THE ROLLER (TORCEDOR) CONSIST OF (FROM LEFT TO RIGHT) A POT OF VEGETABLE GUM (GOMA), TWO CUTTERS (THE FLAT-BLADED CHAVETA AND THE LITTLE DISC-CUTTING CASQUILLO), A WOODEN BOARD (TABLA), FILLER LEAVES, BINDER LEAF AND WRAPPER LEAF, A TEMPLATE (CEPO) AND A GUILLOTINE.

high proportion of *ligero*. Small or thin cigars might well have no *ligero* tobacco at all, depending on the brand.

The *ligador* is responsible for maintaining the consistency of the precise 'recipe' of each brand and size he's responsible for. Filler and binder leaves are combined, in secure conditions, in the blending room according to the proportions ordered by the *ligador*, and are assembled in batches to go to the rollers. The blending department is nicknamed *la barajita* – the pack of cards – because the work of the blenders is rather like shuffling and dealing cards.

The next day, each roller gets enough of the blended leaves to make 50 cigars. There are, typically, two to three hundred rollers in a Havana factory. Until the Cuban Revolution cigar rollers (*torcedores*) were exclusively male, but now most rollers are women (*torcedoras*). The El Laguito factory, an Italianate former mansion, once home to a Cuban aristocrat, which originally opened in the 1960s as a training school for rollers, was the first to use *torcedoras*. Today, all the rollers at the factory, famous for its production of Cohibas, are women. The word *torcedor* rather oddly means twister – a somewhat inaccurate description of their work.

The rollers sit at benches rather like old-fashioned school desks. The walls are covered with revolutionary slogans, messages emphasising the importance of quality, and portraits of Castro, Che Guevara and other national icons. The atmosphere in the large rolling rooms is good

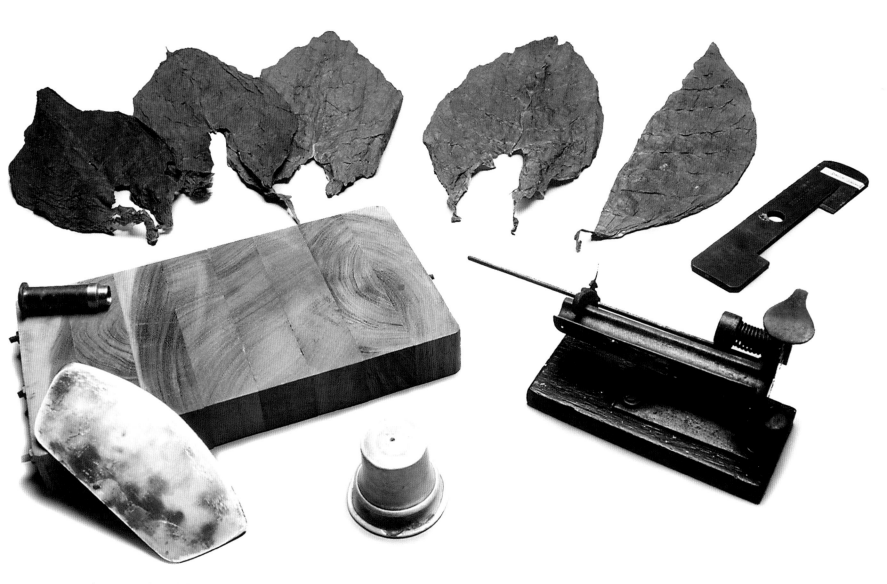

humoured and lively, but the rollers also bring intense concentration and pride to the job. If a visitor comes into the room, he or she is greeted by the noise of all the rollers tapping their flat-bladed cutting tools (*chavetas*) on their tables. The *torcedores* work up to 48 hours a week and are paid piece work: according to the number of cigars they produce. This is typically a few hundred dollars a month. They can smoke as many cigars as they like when they work, and can take up to five cigars home each day.

As they work, the rollers listen to radio programmes, music and extracts from books and newspapers, selected by popular vote, and read aloud by colleagues with fine voices. The readers (*lectoros*) perform from a platform at the front of the room, and are compensated for loss of earnings by a small payment made by each of the other rollers. The tradition, a way of educating workers, and preventing boredom, dates from 1864.

The method of making cigars by hand has also scarcely changed since the mid-19th century, by which time top-quality cigar production had been perfected and standardised. The tools are simple, but the process requires considerable deftness, practice and care.

Preparing the wrapper and blending

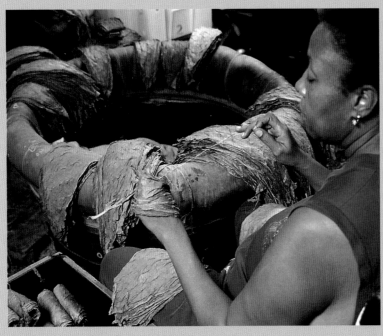

ABOVE: *WRAPPER LEAVES ARE SORTED BEFORE STRIPPING. THE WOMEN PERFORMING THIS IMPORTANT TASK REMOVE THE ENTIRE CENTRAL VEIN OF A LEAF IN ONE DEFT MOVEMENT, LEAVING THE LEAF IN TWO HALVES.*

ABOVE: *BLENDING IS THE PROCESS WHICH DEFINES THE CHARACTERISTICS OF ANY GIVEN BRAND. IN FACT, THE SELECTION OF LEAVES FOR EACH BRAND'S BLEND ACTUALLY STARTS WELL BEFORE THE TOBACCO GETS TO THE FACTORY. THESE DAYS, HAVANA CIGAR FACTORIES (I.E. THOSE PRODUCING HAND-MADE CIGARS FOR EXPORT) ALL MAKE MORE THAN ONE BRAND. SO, AS SOON AS A FACTORY'S MASTER BLENDER (LIGADOR) KNOWS WHICH CIGARS HE WILL NEED TO PRODUCE, HE DECIDES ON EXACTLY WHICH LEAVES HE WILL NEED TO MAKE THEM.*

The roller's art

ABOVE: NOW THE ROLLER COMPLETES THE BUNCH BY ROLLING THE FILLER INTO THE BINDER TO ACHIEVE THE CORRECT DIAMETER FOR THE SIZE (VITOLA) BEING MADE. ROLLING STARTS AT THE FOOT OF THE CIGAR, AND CARE HAS TO BE TAKEN TO MAKE SURE THAT THE FILLER IS EVENLY COMPRESSED THROUGHOUT ITS LENGTH. THE MOUTH END (HEAD) IS THEN SQUARED-OFF USING A SMALL GUILLOTINE.

ABOVE: THE FIRST STAGE OF ROLLING IS TO MAKE A 'BUNCH': THE BODY OF THE CIGAR, CONSISTING OF FILLER AND BINDER. THIS BEGINS BY THE ROLLER (TORCEDOR) LAYING OUT THE TWO (OR SOMETIMES THREE) HALF LEAVES THAT WILL MAKE THE BINDER (CAPOTE) ON A WOODEN BOARD (TABLA) SO THAT THEIR VEINED UNDERSIDES FACE WHAT WILL BECOME THE INSIDE OF THE CIGAR. NEXT, THE ROLLER GATHERS TOGETHER TWO TO FOUR FILLER LEAVES (THE NUMBER DEPENDS ON THE CIGARS'S STRENGTH AND SIZE), EVENLY FOLDING AND ALIGNING EACH ONE TO MAKE SURE THE CIGAR WILL DRAW PROPERLY. THE BUNCH IS THEN PLACED IN A WOODEN MOULD IN ORDER TO CONFIRM ITS SHAPE.

Adding the wrapper and cap

ABOVE: *To add the wrapper the roller lays a half leaf on the tabla; the side with most veins faces upwards, so that the outside of the cigar is as smooth as possible. The roller then trims it to the appropriate size, using the oval chaveta blade.*

ABOVE: *Next the bunch is laid at an angle across the wrapper and rolled using overlapping turns, with the tip of the wrapper starting at the foot of the bunch. The wrapper has to be carefully stretched and smoothed as this is done. After the final turn of the leaf, the wrapper is stuck down using a drop of flavourless and colourless tragacanth vegetable gum. The roller then gently presses and rotates the cigar under the flat part of the cheveta to make sure it is as even as possible.*

ABOVE: *The final stage in rolling a hand-made cigar is to make the cap. First, a piece of tobacco is cut from spare wrapper leaf, and is wound round the head, closing off the open end, and securing the wrapper. Now see right.*

ABOVE: *Next a round piece of wrapper (the size of a small coin) is cut from the leaf trimmings, using an instrument called a casquillo. Now see below left.*

BELOW: *Next, the piece of leaf is wound round the head, closing shut the open end.*

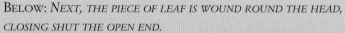

BELOW: *Finally, it is stuck in position using colourless and flavourless natural vegetable gum.*

Opposite THESE CIGARS ARE KNOWN AS FIGURADO. *A CENTURY AGO MOST HABANOS WERE THIS TORPEDO SHAPE. TODAY THE SHAPE IS RARE, EXCEPT IN THE CUABA BRAND (SEE PAGE 74), EVERY SIZE OF WHICH IS POINTED AT BOTH ENDS (DOUBLE FIGURADO).*

Apprenticeship for rollers takes nine months, an indication of how skilled and difficult their craft. The most experienced rollers in the room sit at the front, the least experienced at the back. For details of bunching and rolling, see page 53.

Although the buncher is also the roller in Cuban factories, and sees the cigar through to the end, in other countries, such as the Dominican Republic, the tasks of bunching and final rolling are performed by different specialists, with each buncher usually supplying two rollers. Next, the wrapper and cap are added - see page 55.

There are seven grades of rollers in the Cuban cigar factory. Those in grades one to three, the beginners, perform other tasks in the factory while they sharpen their skills. The least experienced (in grade four) only make cigars up to and including the petit corona size. Those in grade 5 make the corona size and above. Those in grades 6 and 7 (the latter grade being confined to a few star rollers) roll the difficult specialist sizes such as piramides. Rollers are paid according to their grade (those in the highest grades will have had more than 20 years' experience), so the roller's skill is reflected in the eventual cost of a cigar. The system is similar in other countries. That's why smaller sizes are relatively cheap compared with bigger or more unusual ones.

Most skilled rollers can make around a hundred medium-sized cigars a day. But the very best rollers can produce some 150 cigars during an eight-hour day, an average of no more than five minutes a cigar. Although one famous roller was able to make a remarkable 200 Montecristo As in a day, three to four times the rate of his colleagues, very large and unusual sizes are normally produced much more slowly, at about 50 or 60 a day. This, again, is reflected in their price. The work of the rollers is overseen by the workshop manager (*el jefe de galera*), and more directly supervised by top-grade *torcedores,* who check the work of the 30 to 40 people in each team.

HAND MADE OR MACHINE MADE?

*T*HE PROCEDURE described on these pages is the long filler method, and this is the essential difference between hand-made cigars and most of those cheaper cigars made by machine, which normally use shredded tobacco. Some of the very best machine-made cigars (including those produced in Cuba) use long filler, meaning separate leaves arranged along the length of the cigar, but large or specialist sizes can only satisfactorily be made by hand, and only hand-made cigars ensure a cool and even draw.

In the early 1990s, the Cubans launched what they call 'hand finished' machine-made cigars. They are made with long filler, bunched by machine, and have good wrappers and caps similar to hand-mades. But they still can't quite match up. If you're not familiar with a brand, don't be fooled by terms such as 'hand finished'. If a cigar isn't totally hand made, it's not hand made.

The Cubans complicated the definition of hand-made cigars further in the late 1990s, by marketing what is called the *tripa corta*, or short filler method. This was the method used for Cuban country cigars for domestic consumption and, although the cigars are made completely by hand, they use trimmings from the bunches of long-filler cigars, as well as other chopped tobacco. The *torcedor* rolls this filler into whole binder leaves with the help of a flexible mat fixed to his bench, so that he can form a firm bunch. The wrapper is then rolled on in the traditional way. Cigars made in this way used to be called *cazadores* in some Cuban brands. But these cigars, hand made though they might be, can't really be compared to the best cigars made by the long filler method. They're obviously cheaper, however.

Cellophane wrapping on Cuban cigars is a definite sign that they are machine made, but not on non-Cuban brands, many of which, including some of the best, such as Macanudo, are individually wrapped in cellophane.

To add to the confusion, a number of Cuban brands (such as H. Upmann and Punch) have machine-made sizes as well as hand-made ones. And some Cuban brands which were once hand made, and later made only by machine – La Flor de Cano, for instance – are now also made using the *tripa corta* method. The Por Larranaga brand, which was once also discontinued as a hand-made now features not only cigars made by hand using long filler, but also by the *tripa corta* method, *and* by machine. A number of non-Havana brands also have machine-made cigars in their ranges. And some very small sizes bearing famous names, usually identifiable by their lack of caps, normally sold in cardboard cartons, are also machine made.

The quality of leaves used for machine made cigars is normally inferior to the leaves used for hand-mades. The wrappers on completely machine-made cigars gives the best clue of their provenance: they are likely to be coarse, and will sometimes feature protruding veins. They have to be coarser to cope with the rigours of being put on mechanically: quite a different matter to the tender handling of wrappers by a roller. Another pretty good way of telling the difference between hand-mades and all but the best machine-mades is to look at the cap. The caps on machine-mades tend to be noticeably pointed rather than smoothly curved. The cheapest machine-mades often come with no caps at all.

The long filler method is also called the book method. Unfortunately, the only way to check whether or not the method is being used (unless, of course, you are smoking a brand which you know to be hand-made with long filler) is to cut the cigar lengthwise with a razor: the filler leaves should then look like the pages of a book.

Once a roller has finished 50 cigars, he or she uses a coloured ribbon to tie them into a bundle of 50. This is a *media rueda*, or half wheel. These are labelled with the roller's identification number, the type of cigar and the date of manufacture. The majority of these bundles go to be treated against pests in a vacuum fumigation chamber.

QUALITY CONTROL

*B*UT, JUST AS IMPORTANT, a number of bundles made by each roller are removed to be put through checks in the quality control department the following day.

An over-filled or 'plugged' cigar, or a badly constructed one (where the filler leaves are not properly aligned, for instance), will have a frustratingly poor draw and need frequent re-lighting, impairing its flavour. If it is under-filled, it will burn too fast, resulting in a cigar that is hot hold and rough to smoke. Cigars must also look good and be properly stored, so quality control in the factory is essential to the integrity of a brand, and its price.

The percentage of cigars tested varies from brand to brand, and according to the policy of each factory. For the most prestigious brands, such as Cohiba, up to 20 per cent of the output might be checked. For other brands, maybe only 10 per cent of the cigars will be examined. The tests are rigorous and detailed, checking elements such as the

GEO. S. HARRIS & SONS

443 PEARL STREET, NEW YORK CITY.

108-110 RANDOLPH ST., CHICAGO, ILL.

No. 5298. Flap, $18.00 per 1000 net.

ALSO FURNISHED BLANK.

Above EARLY U.S. CIGAR FACTORY NAMED AFTER HENRY VANE, GOVENOR OF MASSACHUSETTS, LATER A LEADING FIGURE IN THE ENGLISH CIVIL WAR.

tightness and smoothness of the wrapper; the finish of the cap; the weight, length and firmness; whether the ends have been cleanly guillotined, and the general appearance. Samples of each roller's work are also regularly taken apart to make sure that their blend is accurate and that they are properly made. Substandard cigars are deducted from the roller's daily quota, and therefore his or her pay.

In 2001, the Cubans started to install state of the art machines to check how cigars draw. The test takes place after the bunch has been pressed in the mould, and before the wrapper is added. The machines are similar to the ones used for many years in the internationally-owed factories of the Dominican Republic. But smaller manufacturers outside Cuba still prefer to do everything by hand.

In Cuba, testing is also done by mouth. A small proportion of cigars in a Havana factory are actually smoked by professional tasters (*catadores*). The *catadores*, themselves tested a couple of times a year, have to report on six criteria, including draw, burning qualities and aroma. There are also specific criteria for individual sizes: the flavour of a *robusto*, or the draw of a *panatela,* for instance. They work in the morning, testing say three to five different cigars at each sitting, by smoking around an inch of each cigar, and freshening their palates with black tea in between each one. This way, the work of all the rollers eventually gets checked. The *catadores* will also recommend adjustments to the blend.

Painstaking quality control, with its attendant wastage, adds to the cost of hand-made cigars. But the very fact that the best cigars are made by hand, with room for human error, is what – even though it makes them much more expensive – gives them such a big edge over machine- mades.

CONDITIONING AND PACKING

After the fumigation chamber (to rid the cigar of pests), cigars are taken to a conditioning room (*escaparte*) and left to rest in cooled, cedar-lined cabinets, each holding up to 18,000 cigars. The idea is to slow down any further fermentation, to remove excess moisture, and to allow flavours to meld. The ambience is strictly controlled at 16-18 C, and 65-70 per cent humidity: both cooler and drier than normal Cuban conditions. The cigars become smokeable after a week. Some brands are packed at this stage, but the best are stored for three weeks more, or longer. In the Dominican Republic, some of the leading brands age their most expensive cigars in this way for several months.

After being cooled, the cigars, in batches of a thousand of each type of brand and size, have to be colour graded. There are around a dozen basic colour classifications, and more than 60 shade categories. The graders (*escogedores*) have to be able to recognize them all and are among the most senior workers in the factory; they work in pairs. One *escogedor* sorts all the cigars in a batch by colour and shade while his colleague then sorts the cigars within each shade, one box-full at a time. The cigars are arranged so that the darkest is on the left, the lightest on the right. This grader also decides which side of the cigar should face upwards. Once the cigars have been colour graded, they go, in their transit boxes, to have their brand bands delicately applied. Then the cigar is returned to its position in the box. All the bands have to be in exactly the same place on each cigar.

Cigar DIRECTORY

Left THE ANILLADORA - OR 'BANDER' -
APPLIES A BAND TO EACH CIGAR AND
PLACES THEM IN THEIR PART-DRESSED BOX.

THIS CAN CLAIM to be the most comprehensive illustrated directory of hand-made cigars ever published. It features an unusually large number of sizes and all are shown life-size. It begins on page 66 with all the Havana (Cuban) brands and continues on page 122 with a large selection of non-Cuban brands. So many brands are now produced outside Cuba that it is impossible, however, to include them all, especially as some come and go. Non-Havana brands that share names with Cuban brands – eg. Honduran Hoyo de Monterreys – are included under the relevant Cuban entries. All brands follow in alpha order.

Cigar Sizes

On mainland Europe, cigar dimensions are normally measured using centimetres or millimetres. But in Britain and the English-speaking markets the thickness of a cigar has traditionally been expressed in terms of its 'ring gauge', measured in ¹⁄₆₄ths of an inch. So if a cigar has a ring gauge of 42, it is ⁴²⁄₆₄ths of an inch in diameter, or 'girth'.

There are a number of basic cigar sizes - such as *panatela*, *robusto* (also called Rothschild), *corona*, double *corona*, *especial*, Lonsdale and Churchill. However: these sizes not only have many variations, but they can vary from brand to brand, and the terms are also sometimes applied in a rather cavalier fashion.

Various classic 'specialist' sizes also exist, such tapering *pyramides* (the Cubans normally spell it *piramide*), *belicosos* (sometimes called "torpedoes") and *figurados* - technically cigars pointed at both ends. The word *figurado* is now used for any unusually shaped cigar, and is pretty much interchangeable with *perfecto*. There can, theoretically, be any combination of length and thickness, but in practice ring gauges for hand-made cigars run from 26 (10.1mm) through to monster cigars, such as the Casa Blanca Jeroboam, with a ring gauge of 66 (26.1mm). And lengths can vary from less than four inches (157mm) to ten inches/254mm (in the case of the Royal Jamaica Ten Downing Street size, for instance). But sometimes cigars have been even bigger. At the time of writing, the Davidoff organization is planning to introduce Esquisitos, designed to be the world's smallest hand made cigar. Some sizes, such as the famous Montecristo A, are very much associated with a particular brand. And many brands add new sizes (or dispense with them) for marketing or production reasons. The number of sizes produced by each brand varies from a handful to literally dozens. In all there are more than 60 hand-made Havana cigar sizes (*vitolas*). In Cuba they all have factory names, most of which aren't normally used commercially. Some of the basic hand-made sizes are listed on the next page, but this table is only for general guidance, and not definitive. Where appropriate, Cuban factory names are given in brackets. Pictured left is a Hoyo de Monterrey Part (one of the largest cigars in our directory) and right, a Ramon Allones Maestro, (one of the smallest cigars in our directory).

A selection of sizes: from left to right, Montecristo A, Hoyo de Monterrey Double Corona, Romeo y Julieta Churchill, Romeo y Julieta Bellicosos, Quintero Panetelas. and Cohiba Robustos.

Name	Length (inches)	Ring Gauge
Montecristo A (Gran Corona)	9 $\frac{1}{4}$	47
Double Corona (Prominente)	7 $\frac{5}{8}$	49
Especial (Laguito No. 1)	7 $\frac{1}{2}$	38
Long Panatela	7	36
Churchill (Julieta 2)	7	47
Lonsdale (Cervante)	6 $\frac{1}{2}$	42
Pyramide (Piramide)	6 $\frac{1}{8}$	52
Corona Extra (Corona Gorda)	5 $\frac{5}{8}$	46
Corona	5 $\frac{5}{8}$	42
Belicoso (Campana)	5 $\frac{1}{2}$	52
Robusto/ Rothschild	5	50
Petit Corona (Mareva)	5	42
Panetela (Laguito No. 3)	4 $\frac{1}{2}$	26
Tres Petit Corona (Perla)	4	40
Demi-Tasse (Entreacto)	3 $\frac{7}{8}$	30

This famous brand was founded around 1901 or 1902 by the J.F. Rocha company, but it didn't really become as internationally well known as it is today until after the Second World War, when the brand (along with La Gloria Cubana) was passed on to the Cifuentes family in 1954 after Jose F. Rocha's death. It had become particularly popular in Britain by the time of Castro's revolution, and production has continued without interruption to this day. It is named after an earlier revolutionary than Fidel Castro, Simon Bolivar, the 19th Century soldier and statesman who fought against Spanish rule and, nicknamed El Libertador, who freed much of South America including Venezuela, Peru and Bolivia from Spain. His portrait (he was apparently much admired by Rocha) appears on both box and bands - although a crest, and not his face, appeared on some pre-Second World War bands.

BOLIVAR

Made in the Partagas factory, which specialises in strong cigars, Bolivars, with their dark wrappers, are still relatively cheap as Havanas go even though prices have recently been raised. But they are also one of the fullest-bodied of Havanas, and definitely not recommended for the beginner or those who like to smoke cigars in the morning. However, many seasoned smokers love them. Although you might expect their rich, earthy, flavour to come from the use of extra *ligero* tobacco, it is actually the fact that more *seco* than *volado* leaf is used in the filler blend that is responsible. Bolivars age particularly well, reaching peak condition in around five years. They are available in most, but not all, countries.

The range available for export has been heavily reduced in the last few years to twelve hand-made sizes - including tubed versions - and two (Belvederes and Chicos) made by machine and identifiable by the fact that they are packaged in cellophane. Even the machine-mades have their fans among Bolivar lovers. The larger sizes (Coronas upwards), in particular, are favourites with connoisseurs of heavy cigars. They have a powerful aroma, good draw, and better construction than the smaller sizes. The longest in the range, the Coronas Gigantes (a Churchill) is an excellent after-dinner cigar. The torpedo-shaped Belicosos Finos are also popular after a heavy dinner; and the Royal Corona (a *robusto*) for a brief, smooth, but powerful smoke after a good lunch. It was called the Prince Charles until 1973. The Petit Corona is one of the most flavour-packed of that size available in any brand. The Inmensas (which isn't as big as the name suggests) is also a popular strong smoke. A series called the Amado Seleccion (C, E and G) were produced for the British importers Joseph Samuel & Son in the 1980s, and was discontinued in 1993, when the company was taken over by Hunters & Frankau. These cigars were the same as the Coronas Extra, Royal Coronas and Coronas Junior. Some people suggest that a number of Bolivar sizes have become milder since the mid-1990s, but they are consistently well made.

There are also Dominican Bolivars on the market. Confusingly, they have very similar packaging, come in ten sizes, and are not particularly special. With pale Connecticut Shade wrappers, Indonesian Jember binder, and Dominican filler, they are much milder than the Cuban version.

THE BOLIVAR GOLD MEDAL - A VERY STRONG CIGAR - HALF OF WHICH WAS WRAPPED IN GOLD-COLOURED FOIL IS A COLLECTORS' ITEM WHICH EXISTED BEFORE THE REVOLUTION AND WAS DISCONTINUED IN 1992. IT HAD A RING GAUGE OF 42 (16.67MM) AND WAS 6 1/2 INCHES (165 MM) LONG.

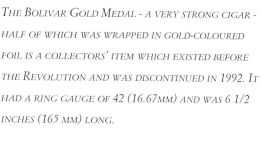

CORONAS GIGANTES: RING GAUGE **47 (18.65 mm)**, LENGTH **178 mm (7 inches)**

BELICOSOS FINOS: RING GAUGE **52 (20.64 mm)**, LENGTH **140 mm (5½ inches)**

ROYAL CORONAS: RING GAUGE **50 (19.84 mm)**, LENGTH **124 mm (4⅞ inches)**

IMMENSAS: RING GAUGE **43 (17.07 mm)**, LENGTH **170 mm (6¼ inches)**

CORONAS EXTRA: RING GAUGE **44 (17.46 mm)**, LENGTH **143 mm (5⅝ inches)**

Coronas: RING GAUGE **42** (16.67 mm), LENGTH **142** mm (5⅝ inches)

Petit Coronas: RING GAUGE **42** (16.67 mm), LENGTH **129** mm (5⅛ inches)

Bonitas: RING GAUGE **40** (15.87 mm), LENGTH **126** mm (5 inches)

Coronas Junior: RING GAUGE **42** (16.67 mm), LENGTH **110** mm (4⅜ inches)

Bolivar Tubos No.1: RING GAUGE **42** (16.67 mm), LENGTH **142** mm (5⅝ inches)

BOLIVAR TUBOS No.2: RING GAUGE **42 (16.67 mm)**, LENGTH **129 mm (5⅛ inches)**

BOLIVAR TUBOS No.3: RING GAUGE **34 (13.49 mm)**, LENGTH **125 mm (5 inches)**

BELVEDERES: RING GAUGE **39 (15.48 mm)**, LENGTH **125 mm (5 inches)**

CHICOS: RING GAUGE **29 (11.51 mm)**, LENGTH **106 mm (4⅛ inches)**

THE BRAND ONCE PRODUCED THE SMALLEST HAND MADE HAVANA CIGAR: THE DELGADO, MEASURING JUST 1.87 INCHES WITH A RING GAUGE OF 20 (7.8MM). AND THE COMPANY ONCE MADE A MINIATURE BOX OF CIGARS FOR A DOLLS HOUSE IN THE ROYAL NURSERY AT WINDSOR. THE TWO CELLOPHANE WRAPPED CIGARS ON THIS PAGE ARE MACHINE-MADE.

$\mathcal{C}$ohiba has been the world's leading cigar brand since it was launched on the international market. Founded in 1966, it was once rumoured to have been Che Guevara's idea, but this is a myth. Cohibas were originally made to be given as exclusive gifts to foreign leaders and diplomats, often with personalized bands. The brand's origins are rather unclear, but the accepted version of events is that cigars privately made, and blended by roller Eduardo Rivera, came to the attention of Fidel Castro through one of his own bodyguards. So impressed was Castro, that he ordered official production of the

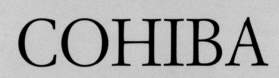

COHIBA

cigars at the El Laguito factory, and put Rivera in charge. At first, the brand had no name, but three sizes of Cohiba - Lancero, Corona Especiale and Panatela - all of them specially created, were launched in 1968. The man most responsible for the brand's development and success was Avelino Lara, once a top-grade roller, and one of Cuba's greatest cigar experts. From 1968 to 1994, Lara ran El Laguito, housed in a former mansion in a smart suburb of Havana. It is still closely associated with Cohiba, although these days various sizes are also produced elsewhere - in the H. Upmann and Partagas factories, for instance.

The cigars went on commercial sale (launched at the Ritz hotel in Madrid) to mark the 1982 soccer World Cup in Spain. Three more sizes - Esplendido, Robusto and the specially created Exquisito - were added in 1989. These sizes are now called the Linea Clasica. Supplies were limited at first, but Cohibas have been on general sale internationally since the early 1990s. Five more sizes, the Siglo series, were launched at Claridge's hotel in London in November 1992, to celebrate the 500th anniversary of

Columbus' great voyage. An additional Siglo size (VI) was added in 2002.

Quality is paramount to the cigar's makers, and the highest standards are strictly applied. Cohibas are made from the best leaves available ("the selection of the selection" as Lara liked to call them), from only five plantations. They take priority over other brands and are made by the best rollers in Cuba. The key to their spicy flavour is that the *ligero* and *seco* filler leaves used in their construction are fermented three times, rather than twice as with other Havanas. This final fermentation, often taking as long as 18 months, takes place in barrels in the factory itself. Some suggest that the extra fermentation means there is nothing to be gained by ageing Cohibas. Others disagree.

The Linea Clasica series is medium to full-bodied, and the Siglo series is somewhat lighter. The *robusto* is the richest, and a favourite, along with the Esplendido, with many. Small sizes, such as the *panatela*, which contain no *ligero* tobacco, are notably milder.

The distinctive flavour of Cohibas is not for everyone, though some seem to choose the brand simply because it is a status symbol, sold at premium prices.

In 2000, Limited Edition Cohibas (see Hoyo de Monterrey entry for details) came on the market. And in 2003 the Seleccion Reserva - five extra smooth sizes made from leaves which have been aged for at least three years - was launched. There are plans to introduce a Gran Reserva selection - using leaves aged for five years. Seleccion Reserva cigars carry an additional black and gold band inscribed "Reserva".

ESPLENDIDOS: RING GAUGE 47 (18.65 mm), LENGTH 178 mm (7 inches)

ROBUSTOS: RING GAUGE 50 (19.84 mm), LENGTH 124 mm (4⅞ inches)

EXQUISITOS: RING GAUGE 33 (13.10 mm), LENGTH 127 mm (5 inches)

PANETELAS: RING GAUGE 26 (10.32 mm), LENGTH 115 mm (4½ inches)

ORIGINAL COHIBA BANDS WERE WHITE (SIMILAR TO THE DAVIDOFF BAND), THE FIRST ONES ON SALE HAD A BRIEFLY HAD A MORE COMPLEX BLACK AND GOLD BAND.

THE CURRENT DESIGN OF SMALL WHITE SQUARES ON A BLACK BACKGROUND ABOVE THE WORD COHIBA HAS CHANGED SUBTLY OVER THE YEARS. THERE WERE THREE WHITE SQUARES ABOVE 'COHIBA' FROM 1982 UNTIL 1992, TWO UNTIL 2003, AND NOW THREE AGAIN, WITH THE WORD 'COHIBA' CURRENTLY IN GOLD RATHER THAN BLACK.

LANCEROS: RING GAUGE **38 (15.08 mm)**, LENGTH **192 mm (7½ inches)**

CORONAS ESPECIALES: RING GAUGE **38 (15.08 mm)**, LENGTH **152 mm (6 inches)**

SIGLO I: RING GAUGE **40 (15.87 mm)**, LENGTH **102 mm (4 inches)**

SIGLO II: RING GAUGE **42 (16.67 mm)**, LENGTH **127 mm (5 inches)**

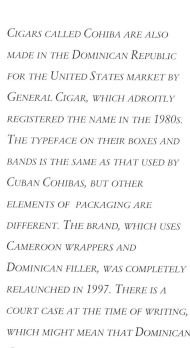

SIGLO III: RING GAUGE **42 (16.67 mm)**, LENGTH **156 mm (6⅛ inches)**

SIGLO IV: RING GAUGE **46 (18.26 mm)**, LENGTH **143 mm (5⅝ inches)**

SIGLO V: RING GAUGE **43 (17.07 mm)**, LENGTH **168 mm (6⅝ inches)**

SIGLO VI: RING GAUGE **52 (20.65 mm)**, LENGTH **149 mm (5⅞ inches)**

CIGARS CALLED COHIBA ARE ALSO MADE IN THE DOMINICAN REPUBLIC FOR THE UNITED STATES MARKET BY GENERAL CIGAR, WHICH ADROITLY REGISTERED THE NAME IN THE 1980s. THE TYPEFACE ON THEIR BOXES AND BANDS IS THE SAME AS THAT USED BY CUBAN COHIBAS, BUT OTHER ELEMENTS OF PACKAGING ARE DIFFERENT. THE BRAND, WHICH USES CAMEROON WRAPPERS AND DOMINICAN FILLER, WAS COMPLETELY RELAUNCHED IN 1997. THERE IS A COURT CASE AT THE TIME OF WRITING, WHICH MIGHT MEAN THAT DOMINICAN COHIBAS WILL BE DISCONTINUED.

CUABA

Cuabas were launched in November 1996, and were originally only available in the UK. The name comes from the old Taino word for a plant noted for its burning qualities. This bush plant still grows on the island today, and was used for lighting cigars at religious ceremonies. The old expression, *Quemar como una Cuaba* (to burn like a Cuaba) is still used by Cuban farmers today.

The range is unusual - all the cigars are *figurados*, tapered at both ends. *Figurados* used to be commonplace in the 19th Century, but had pretty much disappeared by the 1970s, when they were overtaken by straight-sided cigars *(parejos)*. Now they are fashionable again. But few rollers in Cuba had the experience or skill to make them until veteran Carlos Izquierdo Gongalez was asked to train a team in 1995.

Cuabas are made in the Romeo y Julieta factory. The four original sizes were smallish and fairly similar (ring gauges from 42/16.67mm to 46/18.26mm, and lengths from 4 inches/ 101 mm to 5 ¾ inches/145mm). In 2003, the Cubans added two new, bigger sizes - the Salomones and the Distinguidos. Earlier Salomones, produced for special humidors in 1999 have become collectors' items, as have Distinguidos made in 1998 for Millennium Reserve commemorative jars. In late 2001, a limited number of the Diademas size (9 ⅛ th inches/233mm) wrapped in aluminium paper was also produced.

These are excellent medium cigars (the Divinos, the smallest, is also the strongest) with a generally sweet and mellow flavour, appealing to connoisseurs.

Cuabas produced before early 1997 all had irregular shapes, because they were made without a mould. These have since become collectors' items due to their rarity. The cigars became consistent in shape after early 1997, when moulds were introduced.

EXCLUSIVOS: RING GAUGE **46** (18.26 mm), LENGTH **145 mm (5¾ inches)**

GENEROSOS: RING GAUGE **42** (16.67 mm), LENGTH **132 mm 5¼ inches)**

TRADICIONALES: RING GAUGE **42** (16.67 mm), LENGTH **120 mm (4¾ inches)**

DIVINOS: RING GAUGE **43** (17.07 mm), LENGTH **101 mm (4 inches)**

DIPLOMATICOS

The Diplomaticos range, with a carriage and scrolls on its band, was originally created for the French market in 1966. But the range is small, and they aren't that easy to get hold of outside France, although they are exported to several other countries. Though it is sometimes denied, they are essentially Montecristos with a diffcrent label, and as such they are very high quality cigars: rich and subtle, with a fine aroma. They were also cheaper than the equivalent Montecristos, although prices have risen in recent years. Don't confuse them with the Domincan Republic brand Licenciados, which sports a similar logo on its band.

They are very well constructed, and medium to full flavoured, although generally, some claim, rather milder than the equivalent Montecristos. The No.1, No. 2, and No. 3 are particularly good. Although the range is smaller (there are only five types), sizes and numbering are similar to Montecristos. Two other sizes (Nos. 6 and 7) were produced from 1976, but discontinued a few years later.

DIPLOMATICOS No.1: RING GAUGE **42 (16.67 mm)**, LENGTH **165 mm (6½ inches)**

DIPLOMATICOS No.2: RING GAUGE **52 (20.64 mm)**, LENGTH **156 mm (6⅛ inches)**

DIPLOMATICOS No.3: RING GAUGE **42 (16.67 mm)**, LENGTH **142 mm (5⅝ inches)**

DIPLOMATICOS No.4: RING GAUGE **40 (15.87 mm)**, LENGTH **129 mm (5⅛ inches)**

EL REY DEL MUNDO

*N*ot available everywhere, this brand (the name means King of the World) is originally thought to have been founded in 1848 by German Emilio Ohmstedt, and was transferred to the firm of Antonio Allones when he died. However, other accounts suggest that it was founded (or possibly re-registered) by Antonio Allones in 1882. Today, production is controlled by the Romeo y Julieta factory, known for medium-bodied cigars. The brand consists of subtle cigars with fine, oily wrappers (particularly the larger sizes), distinctive aroma, and a mild to medium flavour - the cigar of choice of many informed smokers. Even the bigger sizes are pretty mild, and good for after lunch or daytime smoking.

The range has been adjusted over the last few years, with some sizes discontinued (as well as machine-mades), and the Tainos (Churchill) reintroduced. There are now seven sizes. The *corona* was the favourite cigar of legendary film producer and former owner of 20th Century-Fox, Darryl F. Zanuck, who once owned a plantation in Cuba. During the 1940s and 50s, the brand was the most expensive available.

There is a very good, well made, much fuller-bodied Honduran version of the brand, with many sizes, and completely different names (other than Choix Supreme). They have similar red, gold and yellow bands, but subsitute the word "imported" for "Habana". They have Honduran fillers. The torpedo shaped Flor de Llaneza, named after legendary cigar producer Frank Llaneza of Villazon, is much fancied.

TAINOS: RING GAUGE **47** (18.65 mm), LENGTH **178 mm** (7 inches)

CHOIX SUPREME: RING GAUGE **48** (19.05 mm), LENGTH **127 mm** (5 inches)

CORONAS DE LUXE: RING GAUGE **42** (16.67 mm), LENGTH **142 mm** (5⅝ inches)

PETIT CORONAS: RING GAUGE **42** (16.67 mm), LENGTH **129 mm** (5⅛ inches)

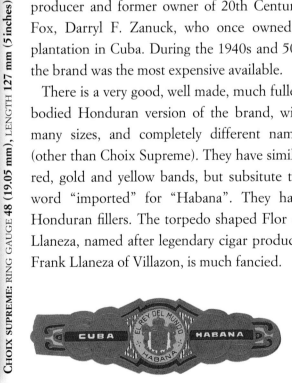

FONSECA

Founded in 1892 by F.E. Fonseca, and registered in 1907, this brand is not very well known outside Spain, where it is a great favourite among knowledgeable smokers. It is, however, now more widely available than it was, and is competitively priced. Early in the 1990s, the Cubans considered discontinuing their hand-made Fonsecas in favour of machine-mades, but decided not to. There are only a few sizes of this brand - three with long fillers (*tripa larga*) and one (Delicias, formerly machine-made) made using the lower quality *tripa corta* method.

Unusually, they come individually wrapped in white tissue paper, with the box featuring both Havana's Morro castle and the Statue of Liberty - a throwback to the good old days before the U.S. embargo - as well as a portrait of F.E. Fonseca. They are excellent light cigars (one of the mildest Havana brands) with a somewhat salty flavour. This makes them ideal cigars for beginners.

The Invictos, discontinued in 2002, had a particularly unusual shape - a normal head, and a curved, pointed foot - of interest to collectors.

Dominican versions of the brand have been on the market since 1965. They are very good, medium-bodied and come with a choice of Connecticut Shade or Broadleaf (*maduro*) wrappers, Mexican binders, and Dominican fillers. They don't come wrapped in tissue, but have nearly identical bands, reading 'Imported' where the Cuban versions say 'Habana'.

FONSECA no.1: RING GAUGE 43 (17.07 mm), LENGTH 162 mm (6⅜ inches)

COSACOS: RING GAUGE 42 (16.67 mm), LENGTH 135 mm (5⅜ inches)

KDT CADETES: RING GAUGE 36 (14.29 mm), LENGTH 115 mm (4½ inches)

KDT CADETES: RING GAUGE 36 (14.29 mm), LENGTH 115 mm (4½ inches)

This celebrated brand was founded in 1865 by Catalan Jose Gener, who had earlier been responsible for the once-famous La Escepcion marque. A wrought-Iron gate in the village of San Juan y Martinez in the Vuelta Abajo announces 'Hoyo de Monterrey De Jose Gener 1860'. It leads to one of Cuba's foremost plantations, once owned by Gener. The *vega fina* still produces some of the finest Havana binder and filler leaf to this day. The word *hoyo* means a hole or a dip in a field - and therefore good drainage, essential to the growth of high quality tobacco leaf.

Hoyo de Monterreys are generally smooth, lightly fragrant and subtle - and too dull for some, but appreciated by real connoisseurs as elegant cigars which can be smoked throughout the day. The brand used to specialize in large cigars, but in 1970, the Le Hoyo series of smaller, more 'accessible' cigars were added to the range.

The most famous Hoyo is the Double Corona. These large, rich but delicate cigars, made at the La Corona factory, were much sought after in the 1990s cigar boom. Shortage of supplies meant that aficianadoes were willing to go to inordinate lengths to get hold of them. They (as well as the recently re-introduced Churchill size, which along with the huge Particulares, was dropped from the range in the mid-1990s) have a different band design to other Hoyos - much bigger and more flamboyant. You should also try the Epicure No. 1 and No. 2 (*robusto*), if you like high-quality mild cigars, though others in the

HOYO DE MONTERREY

range don't always match up. Hoyos don't age all that well, but nor do they normally need to. British design guru, cigar lover and restaurateur Sir Terence Conran, who brought a version of Havana's famous Floridita bar and a Casa del Habano cigar shop to London in 2001, smokes four or five Epicure No. 2s a day, starting with his morning coffee. "They have enough flavour, but aren't too aggressive," he says.

In 2000, the Cubans launched a series of Edicion Limitada or Limited Editions cigars for various leading brands including Hoyo de Monterrey (the others are Cohiba, Montecristo, Romeo y Julieta and Partagas). They use younger, thicker and oilier wrappers from higher up the plant than normal - leaves which were rejected for export in the past. They need to be fermented for longer than normal wrappers, and have to be aged for at least two years in order to avoid an overbearing taste. They are dark, and sometimes have a rather blotchy appearance.

Limited Edition cigars come in unique sizes: Hoyo de Monterrey Particulares (9 ¼ inches/235 mm long, ring gauge 47/18.65mm) and Piramides, for instance; and they sport a second band (identifying them as Edicion Limitada) below the normal one.

There is also a very good Hondurun version of Hoyo de Monterrey, produced by General Cigar (see page 148). They are fine, smooth, full-flavoured cigars - particularly the large sizes such as the President, Churchill, Rothschild and Governors - with a choice of wrapper colour.

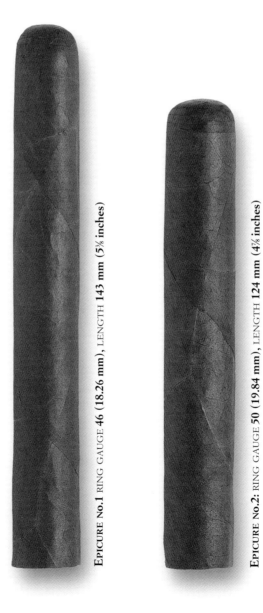

THE LE HOYOS ARE SLIGHTLY SPICIER AND FULLER-BODIED THAN THE REST OF THE RANGE, AND CURRENT LE HOYOS (NOW ONLY THREE OF THEM: THERE WERE SEVEN TYPES NOT LONG AGO) ALL HAVE SLENDER GIRTHS.

DOUBLE CORONAS: RING GAUGE **49 (19,45 mm)**, LENGTH **194 mm (7⅞ inches)**

CHURCHILLS: RING GAUGE **47 (18.65 mm)**, LENGTH **178 mm (7 inches)**

EPICURE No.1 RING GAUGE **46 (18.26 mm)**, LENGTH **143 mm (5⅝ inches)**

EPICURE No.2: RING GAUGE **50 (19,84 mm)**, LENGTH **124 mm (4⅞ inches)**

LE HOYO DES DIEUX: RING GAUGE **42 (16.67 mm)**, LENGTH **155 mm (6⅛ inches)**

THE HOYO DE MONTERREY FACTORY (OWNED BY THE PALICIO FAMILY BEFORE THE REVOLUTION) ORIGINALLY PRODUCED ZINO DAVIDOFF'S CHATEAU SERIES OF CIGARS BEFORE THE CUBAN DAVIDOFF BRAND WAS LAUNCHED, AND LE HOYOS WERE INITIALLY DESIGNED TO RESEMBLE THEM, THOUGH EARLY LE HOYOS WERE NOT PARTICULARLY WELL MADE, AND TENDED TO BURN TOO QUICKLY. THERE ARE NOW ONLY 14 SIZES OF THE BRAND IN THE STANDARD RANGE (INCLUDING LE HOYOS AND ONE TUBED SIZE) WHEREAS THERE WERE 24 A FEW YEARS AGO. MACHINE-MADE SIZES HAVE BEEN DROPPED.

LE HOYO DU ROI: RING GAUGE 42 (16.67 mm), LENGTH 142 mm (5½ inches)

HOYO CORONAS: RING GAUGE 42 (16.67 mm), LENGTH 142 (51/2 inches)

PALMAS EXTRA: RING GAUGE 40 (15.87 mm), LENGTH 140 mm (5½inches)

LE HOYO DU PRINCE: RING GAUGE 40 (15.87 mm), LENGTH 130 mm (5⅛ inches)

SHORT HOYO CORONAS: RING GAUGE 42 (16.67 mm), LENGTH 129mm (5⅛ inches)

CORONATIONS: RING GAUGE 42 (16.67 mm), LENGTH 129 mm (5⅛ inches)

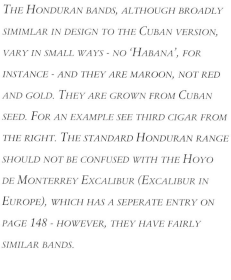

THE HONDURAN BANDS, ALTHOUGH BROADLY SIMIMLAR IN DESIGN TO THE CUBAN VERSION, VARY IN SMALL WAYS - NO 'HABANA', FOR INSTANCE - AND THEY ARE MAROON, NOT RED AND GOLD. THEY ARE GROWN FROM CUBAN SEED. FOR AN EXAMPLE SEE THIRD CIGAR FROM THE RIGHT. THE STANDARD HONDURAN RANGE SHOULD NOT BE CONFUSED WITH THE HOYO DE MONTERREY EXCALIBUR (EXCALIBUR IN EUROPE), WHICH HAS A SEPERATE ENTRY ON PAGE 148 - HOWEVER, THEY HAVE FAIRLY SIMILAR BANDS.

LE HOYO DU GOURMET: RING GAUGE 33 (13.10 mm), LENGTH 170 mm (6¾ inches)

LE HOYO DU DEPUTE: RING GAUGE 38 (15.08 mm), LENGTH 110 mm (4⅜ inches)

LE HOYO DU MAIRE: RING GAUGE 30 (11.91 mm), LENGTH 100 mm (4 inches)

CAFE ROYAL (TUBOS): RING GAUGE 43 (17.07 MM), LENGTH 150 MM (57/8 inches)

PART - EDICION LIMITADES: RING GAUGE 47 (18.65 MM), LENGTH 230.5 MM (9.2 inches)

PIRAMIDES - EDICION LIMITADES: RING GAUGE 52 (20.64 MM), LENGTH 150.3 mm (6 inches)

$\mathcal{H}$. Upmann is one of the best-known of Havana brands, and it is one steeped in history. In the first place, founded in 1844, it is one of the oldest Cuban brands. Some suggest that the precise details of its origins might be rather less clear cut than was formerly thought. However, the accepted version is that it was founded by Herman Upmann, a German banker who moved to Cuba and decided to diversify into cigars. The Upmann banking operation failed in 1922, and the cigar side of the business was taken over by the British cigar firm J. Frankau & Co. J. Frankau sold it to Menendez y Garcia in 1937, who owned it until the Revolution. A new factory opened in central Havana in 1944 to celebrate the brand's centenary. The factory in Calle Amistad, a magnet for cigar-loving tourists, made Upmanns until November 2003, when production moved to a refurbished building in the smart suburb of Vedado.

Among the brand's claims to fame is that it was responsible for introducing the cedar box in the form which is so familiar today. Before that, cigars were sold in bundles or large chests. The word 'brand' itself is thought to come from the fact that the firm's name was actually branded (using a hot iron) on to the boxes. H. Upmann was also responsible for the introduction of the cedar-lined aluminium tube in the 1930s.

Havana Upmanns offer a smooth, mild to medium smoke, ideal for beginners (apart from the biggest sizes), occasional or daytime smokers. But the quality of construction sometimes lets them down (particularly the smaller sizes), leading to overheating. This may be a result of the number of sizes available, some of them identical

H. UPMANN

(the Monarchas and Sir Winston, for instance, or the Petit Coronas and Regalias). The range has been reduced from over 30, but it is still large. There are now some 14 hand-made sizes (including tubed versions), three machine-made sizes sold wrapped in cellophane, and one tubed machine-made (Singulares). The Cubans plan to phase out the machine-mades in the next couple of years. There are also plans for Edicion Limitada Upmanns (see Hoyo de Monterrey entry page 78). Upmanns benefit from ageing.

Dominican Upmanns, made by Altadis, have very similar packaging. The main difference is that non-Cuban labels, bands (red and gold) and tubes read: 'H.Upmann 1844', rather than 'H. Upmann Habana'. The cigars themselves are first class, and generally mild to medium. They come in seven ranges featuring several cigars with similar names and sizes to their Havana counterparts. The basic Dominican range, which is large, comes with Indonesian shade-grown wrappers (the type called TBN), Dominican binders and Dominican and Brazilian fillers. The Vintage series is made with Cameroon wrappers, Nicaraguan binders and fillers from the Dominican Republic, Nicaragua and Peru. The rich Reserve series has Ecuadorian Sumatra wrappers, Connecticut Broadleaf binders and a filler blend from the Dominican Republic, Peru and Nicaragua. The fuller-bodied 2000 range is made from reddish brown Habana 2000 (a specially developed hybrid of Connecticut Shade and Cuban seed tobacco) wrappers, Nicaraguan binders and a Dominican/Brazilian filler blend. Other ranges include the Chairman's Reserve (with Connecticut Shade wrappers), and the Anniversary series.

Bigger sizes such as the Monarcas and Upmann No.2 (a piramide) are particularly satisfactory and fairly punchy cigars, which can be enjoyed after dinner. The Connossieur No 1, although it has a slighly smaller girth than normal, is essentially a robusto, and very good.

MONARCAS: RING GAUGE 47 (18.65 mm), LENGTH 178 mm (7 inches)

MONARCAS: RING GAUGE 47 (18.65 mm), LENGTH 178 mm (7 inches),

SIR WINSTON: RING GAUGE 47 (18.65 mm), LENGTH 178 mm (7 inches)

UPMANN No.2: RING GAUGE 52 (20.64 mm), LENGTH 156 mm (6½ inches)

MAGNUM 46: RING GAUGE 46 (18.26 mm), LENGTH 143 mm (5⅝ inches)

CONNOSSIEUR No.1: RING GAUGE 48 (19.05 mm), LENGTH 127 mm (5 inches)

Upmann boxes feature the royal arms of the 19th Century Spanish King Alfonso XII, as well as 11 gold medals won in international competitions in the 19th Century. They are also carry the words 'This is my Signature' and are signed 'H Upmann'.

MAJESTIC: RING GAUGE 40 (15.87 mm), LENGTH 140 mm (5½ inches)

PETIT CORONAS: RING GAUGE 42 (16.67 mm), LENGTH 129 mm (5⅛ inches)

REGALIAS: RING GAUGE 42 (16.67 mm), LENGTH 129 mm (5⅛ inches)

CORONAS MAJOR: RING GAUGE 42 (16.67 mm), LENGTH 132 mm (5¼ inches)

CORONAS MINOR: RING GAUGE 40 (15.87 mm), LENGTH 117 mm (4⅝ inches)

CORONAS JUNIOR TUBOS: RING GAUGE 36 (14.29 mm), LENGTH 115 mm (4½ inches)

CORONAS JUNIOR: RING GAUGE 36 (14.29 mm), LENGTH 115 mm (4½ inches)

The Cuban Upmann range carries two types of bands: the classic red and gold band, and simpler brown ones not unlike those on Montecristos (a brand once also owned by Menendez y Garcia). The last two cigars on the right are Honduran. The two cellophane wrapped cigars and the tubed cigar shown on this page are machine-made.

EPICURES: RING GAUGE 35 (13,89 mm), LENGTH 110 mm (4⅜ inches)

AROMATICOS: RING GAUGE 42 (16,67 mm), LENGTH 129 mm (5⅛ inches)

BELVEDERES: RING GAUGE 39 (15,48 mm), LENGTH 125 mm (5 inches)

PETIT UPMANN: RING GAUGE 31 (12,30 mm), LENGTH 108 mm (4⅜ inches)

SINGULARES: RING GAUGE 40 (15,87 mm), LENGTH 117 mm (5 inches)

LONSDALE: RING GAUGE 42 (16,67 mm), LENGTH 165 mm (6 ½ inches)

PEQUENOS NO. 100: RING GAUGE 50 (19,84 mm), LENGTH 102 mm (4 inches)

JOSE L PIEDRA

The Piedra family went to Cuba in the 19th Century from Asturias in Spain. They settled near the town of Santa Clara, in the heart of the Vuelta Abajo, in Pinar del Rio province, source of the finest Havana leaves. Jose Lamadrid Piedra founded the brand in 1880. Before long, it was one of the most famous Havanas. Still in the hands of the same family (by then it was run by Jose L. Piedra III), the brand became very popular in the United States in the 1940s and 50s. But, because of that fact, sales fell heavily after the American embargo.

So, this is an old brand – and it has a chequered history. Once hand-made, then discontinued in the early 1990s (very few sizes were made in any case, by then), and then machine bunched and hand finished from 1996 as 'country cigars,' using tobacco from outside the all important Pinar del Rio province. Now it has been re-launched and the tobacco comes from the Vuelta Abajo once more. The cigars are made by the short filler, *tripa corta*, method - albeit by hand. As such, these cigars, though relatively cheap, can't really compete with hand-made, long filler (*tripa larga*) Havanas. There are six sizes altogether, all with dark wrappers, - five of them pretty similar. These are rather basic, robust cigars with a medium to full-bodied flavour, which most connoisseurs are unlikely to try.

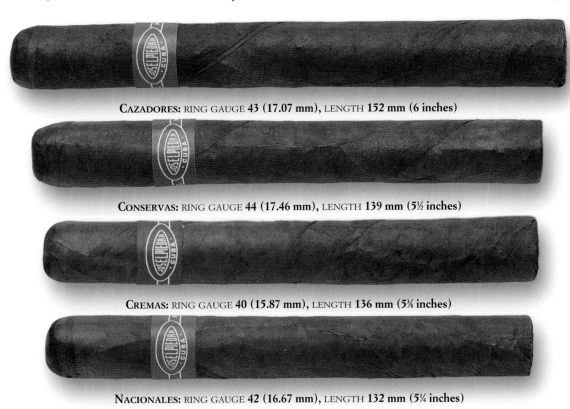

CAZADORES: RING GAUGE **43 (17.07 mm)**, LENGTH **152 mm (6 inches)**

CONSERVAS: RING GAUGE **44 (17.46 mm)**, LENGTH **139 mm (5½ inches)**

CREMAS: RING GAUGE **40 (15.87 mm)**, LENGTH **136 mm (5⅜ inches)**

NACIONALES: RING GAUGE **42 (16.67 mm)**, LENGTH **132 mm (5¼ inches)**

JUAN LOPEZ

Founded by a Spanish businessman, Juan Lopez Diaz, in the 1870s, this brand quickly established itself as a leading Havana name. It was sold to the Cosme del Peso company after Diaz's death in the early years of the 20th Century, and in this new ownership its reputation got even better. It was particularly popular by the time of the Revolution, but the brand wasn't widely distributed after Fidel Castro came to power (it was once only found on sale in Spain) and it isn't easy to find. Devotees used to like Juan Lopez cigars (once called Flor de Juan Lopez) for a very mild, fragrant daytime smoke. The brand had five sizes until the mid-1990s (names such as Patricias, Placeras and Slimaranas), and then only two. The range of names and sizes was changed in the late 1990s. And, more importantly, the blend was also changed. The brand is now definitely medium to full-bodied. There are now five sizes again. I think that the Seleccion No. 1 (*corona gorda*) and No.2. (*robusto*) stand out as the best smokes - but that is a strictly personal opinion.

SELECION No.1: RING GAUGE **46 (18.26 mm)**, LENGTH **143 mm (5⅝ inches)**

SELECION No.2: RING GAUGE **50 (19.84 mm)**, LENGTH **124 mm (4⅞ inches)**

CORONAS: RING GAUGE **42 (16.67 mm)**, LENGTH **143 mm (5⅝ inches)**

PETIT CORONAS: RING GAUGE **42 (16.67 mm)**, LENGTH **129 mm (5⅛ inches)**

LA FLOR DE CANO

Founded in 1884, by two brothers, Tomas and Jose Cano, this was always a fairly rare brand, limited in production, and not widely distributed. It is still only exported to a few countries but, crucially, it has changed its nature. Where once it was a very good, subtle, long filler, hand-made brand (though there were also a number of machine-made sizes) which was known for its mild flavour, it now has only four sizes - none of them special. Two (Selectos and Petit Coronas, shown below) are made using the inferior *tripa corta* (short filler) method, and two (Preferidos and Predilectos, shown below) are machine-made. The flavour is now medium and offers a good balance between flavour and aroma, for a medium price. Old Flor de Canos (from the 1990s or earlier) cigars, such as the Diademas, Short Churchill (a *robusto*) and Gran Corona (a misleading name - it's much shorter) are now collectors' items. Long filler Coronas (actually *petit corona* size) were only discontinued in 2002, so you might find some lingering in shops.

SELECTOS: RING GAUGE **41 (16.27 mm)**, LENGTH **149 mm (5⅞ inches)**

PETIT CORONAS: RING GAUGE **40 (15.87 mm)**, LENGTH **124 mm (4⅞ inches)**

PREFERIDOS: RING GAUGE **36 (14.29 mm)**, LENGTH **127 mm (5 inches)**

PREDILECTOS TUBULARES: RING GAUGE **40 (15.87 mm)**, LENGTH **124 mm (4⅞ inches)**

MONTECRISTO A: RING GAUGE **47 (18.65 mm)**, LENGTH **235 mm (9¼ inches)**

MONTECRISTO No.2: RING GAUGE **52 (20.64 mm)**, LENGTH **156 mm (6⅛ inches)**

MONTECRISTO No.1: RING GAUGE **42 (16.67 mm)**, LENGTH **165 mm (6½ inches)**

MONTECRISTO TUBOS: RING GAUGE **42 (16.67 mm)**, LENGTH **155 mm (6⅛ inches)**

THE BRAND'S EXPORT SALES STILL EASILY BEAT THOSE OF OTHER HAVANAS: INDEED, AT ONE POINT IN THE 1980s, THEY SOLD AS MANY AS ALL OTHER CUBAN BRANDS PUT TOGETHER. THIS HUGE DEMAND HAS LED TO SUSPICIONS - REFUTED BY THE CUBANS - THAT MONTECRISTOS IN SOME MARKETS (SPAIN, FOR INSTANCE) ARE NOT ALL THAT THEY MIGHT BE. THE POPULARITY OF THE BRAND, AND PREMIUM PRICING, MEANS THAT MONTECRISTOS ARE SIGNIFICANTLY MORE EXPENSIVE THAN LESS ILLUSTRIOUS HAVANAS.

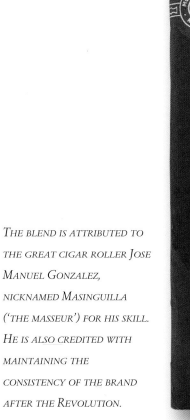

The blend is attributed to the great cigar roller José Manuel Gonzalez, nicknamed Masinguilla ('the masseur') for his skill. He is also credited with maintaining the consistency of the brand after the Revolution.

Montecristo no.3: ring gauge 42 (16.67 mm), length 142 mm (5½ inches)

Petit tub 08: ring gauge 42 (16.67 mm), length 129 mm (5⅛ inches)

Montecristo no.4: ring gauge 42 (16.67 mm), length 129 mm (5⅛ inches)

Montecristo no.5: ring gauge 40 (15.59 mm), length 102 mm (4 inches)

Montecristo especial: ring gauge 38 (15.08 mm), length 192 mm (7½ inches)

THE CUBANS PRODUCED A LIMITED EDITION ROBUSTO, PACKED IN A CERAMIC JAR, FOR THE MILLENNIUM. SUBSEQUENT EDICION LIMITADA (SEE HOYO DE MONTERREY, PAGE 000) MONTECRISTOS WERE A SPECIAL DOUBLE CORONA SIZE IN 2001, AND THE MONTECRISTO C (5 ⅝ INCHES/ 142MM WITH A 46/ 18MM RING GUAGE) IN 2003.

MONTECRISTO ESPECIAL No.2: RING GAUGE 38 (15.08 mm), LENGTH 152 mm (6 inches)

JOYITAS: RING GAUGE 26 (10.32 mm), LENGTH 115 mm (4½ inches)

EDMUNDO: RING GAUGE 52 (20,64 mm), LENGTH 135 mm (5 ⅜ inches)

LEFT A DOMINICAN MONTECRISTO. THE BASIC RANGE ARE GOOD, MEDIUM-BODIED CIGARS. THE No. 1 AND No . 2 ARE SIMIILAR (BUT NOT EXACTLY THE SAME) IN SIZE TO THEIR CUBAN COUNTERPARTS. OTHER SERIES (WITH DIFFERENCES IN PACKAGING, STRENGTH AND BLEND) INCLUDE MONTECRISTO WHITE AND MONTECRISTO PLATINUM.

Partagas, founded in 1845 by Spanish businessman Don Jaime Partagas, is one of the oldest Havana brands still on sale, and one of the best known. The old factory in Havana, near the Capitol building (520, Industria Street), has become a tourist attraction, and is not only one of the most important in Cuba, but pre-eminent in producing fuller-bodied cigars. The brand was sold to Jose Bance in the late 19th Century, and run by the Cifuentes family for most of the 20th Century until the Revolution. It was particularly popular in the 1920s and 30s, and was even mentioned in Evelyn Waugh's 1945 novel, *Brideshead Revisited*.

PARTAGAS

In common with many very old brands, Partagas had a huge range (more than 40 sizes in the late 1990s), many of them machine-mades. It has been reduced, but there are still 20 hand-made types (including three tubed sizes), but now only two machine-mades: Chicos (wrapped in cellophane), and the extraordinary Culebras - essentially three cigars twisted together. Partagas is now the only Havana brand to carry this shape.

Go for the bigger sizes - most of which are excellent - for the full Partagas experience, as some of the smaller ones are sometimes not very well made. The famous Lusitania (a double *corona* measuring 7 ⅝ inches/194mm x 49 ring gauge/19.45mm) is extremely well constructed with an excellent bouquet, and a slightly sweet, full flavour. The Churchill de Luxe and the recently introduced Presidentes (a *figurado*, the only Havana of this type now found outside the Cuaba brand) are also first-class cigars. The Serie D No 4, with its distinctive band, reintroduced to the range in 1975, typifies the qualities of the brand's bigger sizes, and though it has a strong and sometimes rather bitter aftertaste, it is the most popular of Cuban *robustos* among experienced smokers - excellent after a heavy meal. The No. 4 is to be produced in Seleccion Reserva (cigars made with leaves aged for at least three years). A special Edicion Limitada Piramide was produced in 2000.

Partagas cigars are darker than average, usually Colorado Claro, or Colorado, age particularly well.

There is also a Dominican version of the brand manufactured by General Cigar. Dominican Partagas carry the year 1845 on their bands, where the Cuban originals read 'Habana'. The basic range is made with Cameroon wrappers, with binders from Mexico, and a filler blend of Dominican and Mexican tobacco. There is a comprehensive range of sizes, quite a few of them numbered. They are very well-made, smooth, slightly sweet, and medium to full-bodied. The brand is made by General Cigar, originally under the guidance of Ramon Cifuentes and Benjamin Menendez of the famous Cuban cigar families. There are various special series, such as Limited Reserve, which are more expensive than the rest of the brand (which is not cheap) and come with green rather than red bands. Limited Reserve cigars have a blend of filler leaves from the Dominican Republic (*piloto Cubano*) and Mexico, and Cameroon wrappers. They are made in limited qualities, as the name suggests, and specially aged. Partagas Black label cigars are fuller bodied, and the Serie S consists of *figurados* with Cameroon wrappers. The best Dominican Partagas are very good indeed, and, not surprisingly, top sellers in the United States (particularly the No. 1 and No. 10).

LUSITANIAS: RING GAUGE 49 (19.45 mm), LENGTH 194 mm (7⅝ inches)

CHURCHILLS DELUXE: RING GAUGE 47 (18.65 mm), LENGTH 178 mm (7 inches)

PRESIDENTES: RING GAUGE 47 (18.65 mm), LENGTH 158 mm (6¼ inches)

SERIE D No.4: RING GAUGE 50 (19.84 mm), LENGTH 124 mm (4⅞ inches)

*PARTAGAS IS ONE OF THE BEST-
SELLING CUBAN BRANDS - WITH
A LOYAL FOLLOWING AMONG
LOVERS OF EARTHY, FULL-
BODIED CIGARS WITH A
PLEASANT AROMA. THEY
AREN'T, HOWEVER,
RECOMMENDED FOR
BEGINNERS. SOME EXPERTS
SUGGEST THAT THE BRAND AS
A WHOLE HAS BECOME
SLIGHTLY MILDER SINCE THE
MID-1990S.*

THE 8-9-8 (BASICALLY A LONSDALE, BUT SLIGHTLY LONGER), WHICH COMES IN A POLISHED BOX, IS ALSO RECOMMENDED. IT IS ESSENTIALLY THE SAME AS THE PARTAGAS DE PARTAGAS No.1, WHICH COMES IN REGULAR BOXES RATHER THAN 8-9-8 PACKAGING.

8-9-8: RING GAUGE **43** (**17.07 mm**), LENGTH **170 mm** (6¾ inches)

PARTAGAS DE PARTAGAS No.1: RING GAUGE **43** (**17.07 mm**), LENGTH **170 mm** (6¾ inches)

CORONAS: RING GAUGE **42** (**16.67 mm**), LENGTH **139 mm** (5½ inches)

SUPER PARTAGAS: RING GAUGE **40** (**15.87 mm**), LENGTH **139 mm** (5½ inches)

PETIT CORONAS ESPECIALES: RING GAUGE **44** (**17.46 mm**), LENGTH **132 mm** (5¼ inches)

MILLE FLEURS: RING GAUGE **42 (16.67 mm)**, LENGTH **129 mm (5⅛ inches)**

ARISTOCRATS: RING GAUGE **40 (15.87 mm)**, LENGTH **129 mm (5⅛ inches)**

SHORTS: RING GAUGE **42 (16.67 mm)**, LENGTH **112 mm (4⅜ inches)**

PARTAGAS DE LUXE: RING GAUGE **40 (15.87 mm)**, LENGTH **139 mm (5½ inches)**

THE SERIE D GETS ITS NAME BECAUSE THERE WERE ONCE FOUR SERIES (A,B,C AND D) EACH WITH FOUR CIGARS OF DIFFERENT LENGTHS BUT THE SAME GIRTH (SERIE A CIGARS, FOR INSTANCE, ALL HAD A RING GAUGE OF 38/15.08MM). THEY ALL CARRIED BANDS SIMILAR TO THE SERIE D, AND WERE DISCONTINUED IN THE MID-1960s. HOWEVER, THE SERIE D NO. 3 WAS REVIVED FOR A LIMITED EDITION (EDICION LIMITADA) IN 2001, AND THE NO. 2 IN 2003.).

The Coronas are well-made and flavourful. The Serie du Connaisseur (Nos. 1, 2, and 3) are much better made than many slim cigars and burn well.

Coronas Senior: RING GAUGE 44 (17.46 mm), LENGTH 132 mm (5¼ inches)

Coronas Junior: RING GAUGE 40 (15.87 mm), LENGTH 117 mm (4⅝ inches)

Serie du connaisseur No.1: RING GAUGE 38 (15.08 mm), LENGTH 192 mm (7½ inches)

SERIE DU CONNAISSEUR No.2: RING GAUGE 38 (15.08 mm), LENGTH 166 mm (6½ inches)

SERIE DU CONNAISSEUR No.3: RING GAUGE 35 (13.89 mm), LENGTH 143 mm (5⅝ inches)

PRINCESS: RING GAUGE 35 (13.89 mm), LENGTH 127 mm (5 inches)

HABANEROS: RING GAUGE 39 (15.38 mm), LENGTH 124 mm (4⅞ inches)

THE CUBANS INTEND TO MAKE THE BRAND FULLY HAND-MADE IN THE NEAR FUTURE: A GOOD IDEA, AS IN THE PAST, PARTAGAS MACHINE MADES WERE UNSATISFACTORY BY CUBAN STANDARDS.

The Coronas are well-made and flavourful. The Serie du Connaisseur (Nos. 1, 2, and 3) are much better made than many slim cigars and burn well. The cigar on the far right is an example of a Dominican Partagas made by General Cigars. The other two cigars are made in Cuba but are machine-made.

CULEBRAS: RING GAUGE 39 (15.38 mm), LENGTH 145 mm (5¾ inches)

CHICOS: RING GAUGE 29 (11.51 mm), LENGTH 106 mm (4⅛ inches)

LIMITED RESERVE ROYALE RING GAUGE 43 (17.07 mm), LENGTH 170 mm (6¾ inches)

POR LARRANAGA

This is the oldest Havana brand still being produced (founded in 1834 by Ignacio Larranaga) and, in its time, one of the most famous. It was mentioned, for instance, in Kipling's late 19th Century poem, *The Betrothed* (...There's peace in a Larranaga). But it is now a shadow of its former self. Its great days were those of the celebrated Larranaga Magnum, discontinued in the 1970s.

The range consisted of only four hand-made sizes in the early 1990s, as well as half a dozen machine-mades (the company was the first to make cigars by machine). Hand-made versions of the brand were then discontinued, and it became a totally machine-made marque. Now it has been re-jigged in a rather bizarre way, with four sizes: the long filler Monte Carlo, the short filler (*tripa corta*) Panatelas, and the machine-made (and cellophane wrapped) Lolas en Cedro (encased in cedar), and Juanitos. The flavour is now mild to medium, when once the brand was known for its dark, reddish, oily wrappers and a rich, powerful medium to full-bodied flavour

There are first-class cigars using the same name as the Havana brand (as well as very similar bands) made in the Dominican Republic by Altadis one of which is illustrated at the bottom. They are mild to medium in flavour, but rich and extremely well-made with Connecticut Shade wrappers, and Dominican binders and fillers. The Fabuloso (essentially a Churchill) is worth trying.

MONTE CARLO: RING GAUGE **33 (13.10 mm)**, LENGTH **159 mm (6¾ inches)**

PANETELAS: RING GAUGE **37 (14.68 mm)**, LENGTH **127 mm (5 inches)**

LOLAS EN CEDRO: RING GAUGE **42 (16.67 mm)**, LENGTH **129 mm (5⅛ inches)**

FABULOSOS: RING GAUGE **50 (19,84 mm)**, LENGTH **178 mm (7 inches)**

Punch is one of the oldest Havana brand still in production, founded in 1840 by Manuel Lopez of Juan Valle & Co. (although some accounts suggest that it was registered by a German called Stockman, and was sold to Lopez in 1884). Lopez's name still appears on both the bands and box. It was later owned (around 1930) by the Palicio company and made at the Hoyo de Monterrey factory. Fernando Palicio, who was also responsible for the production of La Escepcion and Belinda, among others, was crucial in popularising the half *corona* size (Petit Punch), particularly in Britain. Production continued without interruption after the Revolution, and by the 1970s, Punch was one of the most popular of Havana brands, although it was never exported everywhere, and is still unavailable in some countries.

It is one of the best known and most widely available Cuban brands. It used to have a huge range of sizes (around 40 in the late 1990s), many of them machine made, and mostly produced at the La Corona factory (Fernando Roig to give it its post- Revolution name). The range is still big, but now there are fourteen hand-made sizes, including four in tubes, and two (Belvederes and Cigarrillos) machine-made and wrapped in cellophane. There are plans to discontinue the machine-made sizes. The brand was originally aimed at the British market: hence the name - either taken from the famous humorous magazine, Punch, or the puppet character after which the magazine was named. The figure of Mr Punch, smoking a cigar, is still a feature of the brand's boxes.

Punch cigars are mild to medium, and slightly sweet in flavour. At their best, they are very good, and have a notable bouquet and a spicy aroma. They are cheaper than many Havanas and appeal to many beginners and occasional smokers. Perhaps, as a result, they are disdained by some who ought to know better. They may have their reasons, however, in that with such a large range, quality is sometimes bound to waver. So stick to large sizes such as the rich Punch Punch (which ages well), Churchill and the Double Corona. The Punch blend has managed to stay consistent over the years and is dependable.

PUNCH

There is also a Honduran Punch brand, created by Frank Llaneza of Villazon (now a subsidiary of General Cigar), which started production as long ago as 1969. But luckily, though the packaging (particularly aluminium tubes) is similar, the names of the cigars mostly differ from their Havana equivalents. The Honduran Punch brand, offers a range of fourteen sizes of very well made cigars. The standard line delivers a typically rich, full, Honduran flavour (the filler blend is a mixture of Honduran, Nicaraguan and Dominican leaf; with Connecticut Broadleaf binders and Sumatra seed wrappers from Ecuador). There is a choice of wrapper colour (including *maduro*) in many sizes. A number of sizes are sold in tubes. The Punch Gran Puro range is full-bodied, and uses all-Honduran tobacco, whilst the Deluxe line (created by Estelo Padron) and Gran Cru lines offer more subtle, but equally rich pleasures. The Deluxe series is full-bodied, whilst the Gran Cru line (with Honduran, Nicaraguan and Dominican Piloto Cubano filler, Connecticut Broadleaf binders and Connecticut shade wrappers) is medium, mellow, and the flagship of the brand.

Many Punch cigars with different names used to have the same, or very similar, sizes. There used to be no fewer than six coronas gordas (slightly fatter and longer than average coronas) - Nectares No.2, Selecion de Luxe No. 1, Black Prince Super Selection No.2, Royal Selection No. 11 and Punch Punch. The first two were discontinued in the 1980s, and the next two in 2002. Now only the last two remain in the range.

Double coronas: RING GAUGE 49 (19.45 mm), LENGTH 194 mm (7⅝ inches)

Churchills: RING GAUGE 47 (18.65 mm), LENGTH 178 mm (7 inches)

Churchills: RING GAUGE 47 (18.65 mm), LENGTH 178 mm (7 inches)

Punch punch: RING GAUGE 46 (18.26 mm), LENGTH 143 mm (5⅝ inches)

Royal selection no.11: RING GAUGE 46 (18.26 mm), LENGTH 143 mm (5⅝ inches)

Super selection no.1: RING GAUGE 42 (16.67 mm), LENGTH 155 mm (6⅛ inches)

The famous Macanudo brand, originally made in Jamaica by the Palicios, was an off-shoot of Punch. Macanudo was once the name of a popular Punch size (see Directory entry).

Coronas: ring gauge 42 (16.67 mm), length 142 mm (5⅝ inches)

Petit coronas del Punch: ring gauge 42 (16.67 mm), length 129 mm (5⅛ inches)

Royal selection no.12: ring gauge 42 (16.67 mm), length 129 mm (5⅛ inches)

Petit Punch: ring gauge 40 (15.87 mm), length 102 mm (4 inches)

Royal coronations: ring gauge 43 (17.07 mm), length 145 mm (5¾ inches)

Coronations: ring gauge 42 (16.67 mm), length 129 mm (5⅛ inches)

THE BRAND ACHIEVED POSSIBLY THE BIGGEST SINGLE CIGAR SALE OF ALL TIME WHEN THE BRITISH IMPORTERS MELBOURNE HART ORDERED SEVEN MILLION CIGARS TO BE DISTRIBUTED TO BRITISH SOLDIERS FIGHTING ON THE WESTERN FRONT IN WORLD WAR I. THE LAST TWO CIGARS ON THE RIGHT ARE HONDURAN. THE TWO CELLOPHANE WRAPPED CIGARS SHOWN ON THIS PAGE ARE MACHINE-MADE.

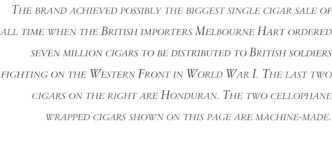

PETIT CORONATIONS: RING GAUGE 40 (15.87 mm), LENGTH 117 mm (4⅝ inches)

MARGARITAS: RING GAUGE 26 (10.32 mm), LENGTH 121 mm (4¾ inches)

BELVEDERES: RING GAUGE 39 (15.48 mm), LENGTH 125 mm (5 inches)

CIGARRILLOS: RING GAUGE 29 (11.51 mm), LENGTH 106 mm (4⅛ inches)

SUPERIORES DELUXE: RING GAUGE 48 (19,05 mm), LENGTH 142 mm (5 ½ inches)

MONARCAS: RING GAUGE 48 (19,05 mm), LENGTH 170 mm (6 ¾ inches)

QUAI D'ORSAY

The Quai d' Orsay brand, as the name suggests, was created for the sophisticated French market in 1973. The Quai d'Orsay is an area of Paris bordering the left bank of the Seine, and home to the French foreign ministry as well as - significantly - the SEITA state tobacco monopoly at the time. The brand is exported to other countries, but is most easily found in France. The four, long-filler, completely hand-made sizes are mild and have wrappers which are light brown (*claro*) or mid-brown (*colorado claro*). These are distinguished cigars with a slightly sweet and spicy flavour. Packaged and banded in a simple decorative style, they are all well worth trying.

IMPERIALES: RING GAUGE **47 (18.65 mm),** LENGTH **178 mm (7 inches)**

PANETELAS: RING GAUGE **33 (13.10 mm),** LENGTH **178 mm (7 inches)**

GRAN CORONA: RING GAUGE **42 (16.67 mm),** LENGTH **155 mm (6⅛ inches)**

GRAN CORONA: RING GAUGE **42 (16.67 mm),** LENGTH **155 mm (6⅛ inches)**

QUINTERO

A robust smoke, but not a particularly old or distinguished brand. It was originally founded in the 1920s on the south coast of Cuba by Augustin Quintero, and his four brothers, in the city of Cienfuengos (mentioned on the label) and, as such, didn't qualify as a Havana until 1940, when the factory moved to the capital and Vuelta Abajo tobacco started to be used. The main market used to be Spain, but the brand is now widely distributed. Although there were some hand-made sizes until the 1970s, many Quinteros used to be machine made. By the early 1990s, the brand was completely machine-made, but some Quinteros also came in machine-bunched and 'hand finished' versions. It used to be a large range, but now there are only five sizes. Four of the five are made by the *tripa corta* (hand-made, but using inferior short filler) method, and one, the Puritos, is machine-made and cellophane wrapped. These are cheap cigars, as Havanas go, and by no means special, although they do appeal to some. The hand-made sizes are all fairly similar. They are medium-bodied in flavour.

BREVAS: RING GAUGE **40 (15.87 mm)**, LENGTH **139 mm (5½ inches)**

NACIONALES: RING GAUGE **40 (15.87 mm)**, LENGTH **139 mm (5½ inches)**

PANETELAS: RING GAUGE **37 (14.29 mm)**, LENGTH **127 mm (5 inches)**

LONDRES EXTRA: RING GAUGE **40 (15.87 mm)**, LENGTH **124 mm (4⅞ inches)**

The name of this brand, founded by Spanish aristocrat Marquez Rafael Gonzalez in the late 1920s or early 1930s, has changed slightly over the years. It was originally called La Flor de Marquez, then (after it was acquired by the Rey del Mundo company) Flor de Rafael Gonzalez. Now it is normally referred to as Rafael Gonzalez, rather than given its full name (which appears on both band and boxes, along with the word 'Marquez'). The brown and white bands are very similar to Montecristo's.

Rafael Gonzalez cigars reek, in every sense of the word, of class. They are particular favourites of discerning smokers and have always had a high reputation (they were praised by Zino Davidoff, for instance, in *The Connoisseur's Book of the Cigar*, published in 1967). They have the added attraction of being sold at medium prices. They are very well made, burn well, and though mild, have a smooth, rich but subtle flavour, and a complex aroma.

Try the Lonsdale 165 mm/6 ½ inches long, with a ring gauge of 42/16.67mm), named after, and created for, the British sporting aristocrat, Lord Lonsdale. The Corona Extra and Petit Corona are equally good. Even the Cigarrito, with its very slim ring gauge of 26/10.32 mm is a good smoke. Beginners can do no better than start with

RAFAEL GONZALEZ

this brand, and women smokers might well find the mild flavour and the elegant smaller cigars such as Slenderellas - with an unusually high quality for their size - very attractive. The number of models has been reduced from nine a few years ago (with the Petit Lonsdale, Tres Petit Lonsdale and DemiTasse no longer available) and there are currently six long filler sizes, and one, Panatela Extra (shown on page 109), made by the *tripa corta* method. The brand is only available in some countries. It is mainly made in the Romeo y Julieta factory (otherwise known as the *Briones Montoto* after the Revolution), where its sister brand, El Rey del Mundo, is also made. Rafael Gonzalez were originally created for the British market, and the box reads (in English): 'These cigars have been manufactured from a secret blend of pure Vuelta Abajo tobaccos selected by the Grandee of Spain. For more than 20 years this brand has existed. In order that the Connoisseur may fully appreciate the perfect fragrance they should be smoked either within one month of the date of shipment from Havana or should be carefully matured for about one year.' Lord Lonsdale was a great cigar lover and his portrait (a photograph) once adorned the inside of the lid, as well as the side of the box, but was dropped in the mid-1980s.

Coronas extra: ring gauge 46 (18.26 mm), length 143 mm (5⅝ inches)

Lonsdales: ring gauge 42 (16.67 mm), length 166 mm (6½ inches)

Petit coronas: ring gauge 42 (16.67 mm), length 129 mm (5⅛ inches)

Slenderellas: ring gauge 28 (11.11 mm), length 175 mm (6⅞ inches)

Panetelas: ring gauge 34 (13.49 mm), length 117 mm (4⅝ inches)

Cigarritos: ring gauge 26 (10.32 mm), length 115 mm (4½ inches)

Panetelas extra: ring gauge 37 (14.68 mm), length 127 mm (5 inches)

The second oldest Havana brand still in existence, founded in 1837, by Ramon Allones, an immigrant to Cuba, from Galicia in Spain, and his brother Antonio. Allones was the first cigar manufacturer to use lithographic labels to decorate cigar boxes. The brand's colourful boxes, which used to be gold until the 1970s, still brandish the Spanish royal coat of arms - now on a bright green background. The brand also pioneered the 8-9-8 form of packaging, in which the box is deeper than normal, often varnished, and where the cigars are arranged with eight at the bottom, nine in the middle row, and eight in the top row.

Regrettably, the brand is now shadow of what it once was. Ramon Allones (made in the Partagas factory since 1927) used to be the first choice of many keen smokers of full-bodied cigars. There was a small but interesting range of eight hand-made sizes in the 1990s (as well as a number of machine mades). But there are now only three hand made sizes, and three machine mades (Mille Fleurs, Belvederes and the oddly named Bits of Havana shown on page 111) with individual cellophane wrappings. However, even though there are so few to choose from, with their dark, high quality wrappers, the hand made cigars have a pronounced aroma, burn well and are very well constructed - the Gigantes (a double *corona*) and Specially Selected (a *robusto* introduced in around 1980) in particular. Both offer an intense smoke after a big meal. They also age very well.

Ramon Allones bands used to be green and white, but have been red white and gold since the early 1970s, with the exception of a few sizes. A version of the old band is currently sported by the (machine-made) Bits of Havana. The Ramon Allones range is medium priced, but only available in a few countries.

Discontinued hand-made Ramon Allones include Club Coronas, Allones No.1, Allones Extra, Private Stock and Ideals de Ramon, all of which were stopped in the 1970s. Palmitas, Petit Coronas, Ramondos and Coronas were all three discontinued in the 1980s and the 1990s. There was also a selection of five sizes produced for Dunhill until 1982, when Dunhaill started to make its own-brand Havanas.

Dominican Ramon Allones - with completely different names - have been produced by General Cigar since the late 1970s. Originally developed by Ramon Cifuentes, they used to have medium to dark Cameroon wrappers, Mexican binders and fillers blended from Dominican, Jamaican and Mexican tobacco. They were well constructed, and mild to medium in flavour. The blend was changed not long ago, under the direction of Daniel Nunez, and now Dominican Ramon Allones are richer and fuller-flavoured than before, using specially-grown Dominican La Vega Especial wrappers, Connecticut Broadleaf binders, and a blend of Nicaraguan *ligero* and Dominican *piloto Cubano* (Cuban seed) *ligero*. The range has been considerably reduced in size, and now consists entirely of cigars with large ring gauges. Their names differ from the original Dominican versions.

RAMON ALLONES

GIGANTES: RING GAUGE 49 (19.45 mm), LENGTH 194 mm (7⅞ inches)

SPECIALLY SELECTED: RING GAUGE 50 (19.84 mm), LENGTH 124 mm (4⅞ inches)

SMALL CLUB CORONAS: RING GAUGE 42 (16.67 mm), LENGTH 110 mm (4⅜ inches)

MILLE FLEUR: RING GAUGE 42 (16.67 mm), LENGTH 129 mm (5⅛ inches)

BELVEDERES: RING GAUGE 39 (15.48 mm), LENGTH 125 mm (5 inches)

BITS OF HAVANA: RING GAUGE 29 (11.51 mm), LENGTH 106 mm (4⅛ inches)

MAESTRO: RING GAUGE 54 (21,44 mm), LENGTH 140 mm (5,½ inches)

*N*ow among the most famous and widely distributed of Havana brands, but originally founded in 1875 to produce cigars only for the Cuban domestic market. Named after Shakespeare's play, the brand's international success came thanks to 'Pepin' Rodriguez Fernandez. The former manager of the Cabanas cigar factory, he resigned in 1903 when it was about to be taken over by American Tobacco, and used his savings to buy the obscure Romeo y Julieta factory, then owned by Rodriguez, Arguelles y Cia, whose name still appears on bands. Through his own tireless - not to say obsessive - efforts travelling the world, and those of his staff (senior managers shared 30 per cent of the profits) Romeo y Julieta became the world's leading brand in just two years. As a result he, and his 1,400 workers, had to move to a larger factory (called Briones Montoto post-Revolution), where the brand is made to this day.

As part of Fernandez's marketing and promotional efforts, his factory at one time produced as many as 20,000 different bands to adorn the cigars of heads of state, celebrities and leading clients. Before he died in 1954, he named his biggest cigar in honour of Winston Churchill. He had earlier named cigars of the same size after the Prince of Wales (later Edward VII) and the French First World War leader, Georges Clemenceau. This medium-priced brand is particularly popular in Britain.

Pepin's devotion to his brand was considerable. He named a racehorse Julieta, and attempted to buy the supposed house of Capulet in Verona. He didn't manage that, but was allowed to have a stall under the balcony, where each visitor, until 1939, was given a free cigar to commemorate the ill-starred lovers and, of course, to promote the brand. In the 1940s and 50s, the brand branched out into *figurados* - which were discontinued in the 1960s and 70s. Romeo y Julieta also produced Dunhill Seleccion cigars for Alfred Dunhill Ltd. until1982.

As with other old brands, the Romeo y Julieta range used to be vast: more than 40 shapes and sizes, including machine-mades. Nowadays, the machine-mades have been discontinued and, although the range has been reduced, there are still 22 sizes, including four in tubes - so that Romeo y Julieta is still the biggest Cuban hand-made, long-filler brand. Many Romeo y Julietas are excellent, classic cigars but, as always with such a big range, and high level of production, second only to Montecristo, not every cigar is going to be up to scratch. In general, Romeo y Julietas are a mild to medium smoke, though the Churchill size, with its gold band (all the others, apart from the Cedros De Luxe series- which are gold on green - have red bands) is fuller flavoured with an impressive aroma - though you can't expect the tubed version to be so well matured. All Romeo y Julietas age well. In 2000, the Exhibicion No 2 was created for a Limited Edition, followed by a special Edicion Limitada Robusto in 2001, and an equally unique Limited Edition Hermoso No. 1 165 mm (6 ½ inches) x 48 ring gauge/19mm) was produced.

ROMEO y JULIETA

CHURCHILLS: RING GAUGE 47 (18.65 mm), LENGTH 178 mm (7 inches)

CHURCHILLS: RING GAUGE 47 (18.65 mm), LENGTH 178 mm (7 inches)

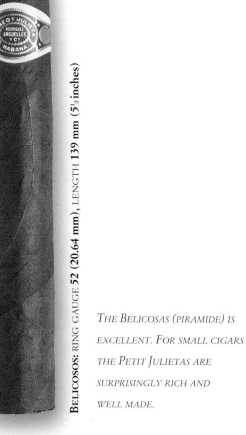

EXHIBICION No.3: RING GAUGE 46 (18.26 mm), LENGTH 143 mm (5⅝ inches)

BELICOSOS: RING GAUGE 52 (20.64 mm), LENGTH 139 mm (5½ inches)

*THE BELICOSAS (PIRAMIDE) IS
EXCELLENT. FOR SMALL CIGARS
THE PETIT JULIETAS ARE
SURPRISINGLY RICH AND
WELL MADE.*

EXHIBICION NO.4: RING GAUGE **48** (**19.05 mm**), LENGTH **127 mm** (**5 inches**)

CAZADORES: RING GAUGE **43** (**17.07 mm**), LENGTH **162 mm** (**6⅜ inches**)

CORONAS: RING GAUGE **42** (**16.67 mm**), LENGTH **139 mm** (**5½ inches**)

PETIT CORONAS: RING GAUGE **42** (**16.67 mm**), LENGTH **129 mm** (**5⅛ inches**)

MILLE FLEUR: RING GAUGE **42** (**16.67 mm**), LENGTH **129 mm** (**5⅛ inches**)

REGALIAS DE LONDRES: RING GAUGE 40 (15.87 mm), LENGTH 117 mm (4⅝ inches)

TRES PETIT CORONAS: RING GAUGE 40 (15.87 mm), LENGTH 117 mm (4⅝ inches)

PETIT PRINCES: RING GAUGE 40 (15.87 mm), LENGTH 102 mm (4 inches)

CEDROS DE LUXE No.1: RING GAUGE 42 (16.67 mm), LENGTH 166 mm (6½ inches)

CEDROS DE LUXE No.2: RING GAUGE 42 (16.67 mm), LENGTH 139 mm (5½ inches)

THE CEDROS DE LUXE RANGE,
BELOW RIGHT, WRAPPED IN
CEDAR, ARE ALL VERY GOOD,
PARTICULARLY THE NO. 2. THE
CORONA IS ALSO A GOOD
CIGAR; AND THE ROBUSTO-
SIZED EXHIBICION NO. 4 IS THE
CHOICE OF MANY
CONNOISSEURS FOR A
SATISFYING SMOKE AFTER A
FULL MEAL.

CEDROS DE LUXE No.3: RING GAUGE 42 (16.67 mm), LENGTH 129 mm (5⅛ inches)

CORONITAS EN CEDRO: RING GAUGE 40 (15.87 mm), LENGTH 129 mm (5⅛ inches)

ROMEO No.1: RING GAUGE 40 (15.87 mm), LENGTH 139 mm (5½ inches)

ROMEO No.2: RING GAUGE 42 (16.67 mm), LENGTH 129 mm (5⅛ inches)

ROMEO No.3: RING GAUGE 40 (15.87 mm), LENGTH 117 mm (4⅝ inches)

OTHER NON-HAVANA ROMEO Y JULIETAS: THE BASIC MILD TO MEDIUM 1875 RANGE COMES WITH INDONESIAN TBM SHADE-GROWN WRAPPERS, DOMINICAN BINDERS AND FILLERS, AND SEVERAL NAMES (INCLUDING CHURCHILL) SIMILAR TO THEIR CUBAN COUNTERPARTS. THE RESERVE MADURO SERIES, AS THE NAME SUGGESTS, ARE FULLER-BODIED DARK CIGARS WITH BLACK LABELS, CONNECTICUT BROADLEAF WRAPPERS, NICARAGUAN BINDERS, AND A FILLER BLEND OF NICARAGUAN, PERUVIAN AND DOMINICAN LEAVES. THE ANIVERSARIO SERIES (WITH BLACK BANDS) IS RICHER AND HAS ECUADORIAN SUMATRA WRAPPERS, CONNECTICUT BROADLEAF BINDERS AND A FILLER BLEND FROM PERU, THE DOMINICAN REPUBLIC AND NICARAGUA. RESERVA REAL CIGARS HAVE ECUADORIAN CONNECTICUT SHADE WRAPPERS, NICARAGUAN BINDERS AND DOMINICAN/NICARAGUAN FILLERS.

BELVEDERES: RING GAUGE 39 (15.48 mm), LENGTH 127 mm (5 inches)

SPORTS LARGOS: RING GAUGE 35 (13.89 mm), LENGTH 117 mm (4⅝ inches)

PETIT JULIETAS: RING GAUGE 30 (11.91 mm), LENGTH 102 mm (4 inches)

THERE ARE ALSO DOMINICAN REPUBLIC VERSIONS OF ROMEO Y JULIETA (ONCE ALSO MADE IN HONDURAS), WITH SIMILAR BOX, TUBE AND BAND DESIGNS (INCLUDING THE CHURCHILL-TYPE GOLD BAND), BUT DIFFERENT TEXT, ARE MADE BY ALTADIS. THERE ARE SEVERAL RANGES. AN EXAMPLE FROM ONE (A PETIT NUMERO DOS) IS SHOWN RIGHT. FOR MORE INFORMATION ON NON-HAVANA ROMEO Y JULIETAS, SEE ABOVE.

These cigars were only exported to Britain before the 1990s. Now they are available in several countries, but are not easy to find. This is partly because they are produced in limited quantities in the Romeo y Julieta (Briones Montoto) factory. That's a shame because these are top-quality full-bodied cigars for the discerning smoker, favourites in times gone by with figures such as Frank Sinatra and James Coburn, which deserve to be appreciated by a wider public.

The brand was only registered around 1940 by the then apparently British-owned Zamora y Guerra company, and exclusively created for the United Kingdom importers, Nathan Silverstone and Michael de Keyser. The association was continued by Cubatabaco after the Revolution, although not many cigars were made until fairly recently when the brand's export share among Havanas almost doubled between 2000 and 2002 - to a higher level than much better-known brands such as Bolivar (page 66).

There are two theories about how the romantic brand name name originated. The one that is most generally accepted is that the brand was named after Thornton Wilder's 1927 novel *The Bridge of San Luis Rey,* or the popular 1944 film of the book - which starred Akim Tamiroff and Alla Nazimova. The other is that it came from the town of San Luis in the heart of the Vuelta Abajo, the area where Cuba's finest tobacco is grown. Maybe it's a bit of both.

SAINT LUIS REY

The wrappers on Saint Luis Reys are of the highest quality : smooth, oily and dark. The flavour of the cigars is intense, but much subtler than better-known full-bodied brands such as Partagas or Bolivar. And they have a superb, distinctive aroma. There used to be nine sizes at one time (including the torpedo-shaped Pyramide No.1, discontinued in the 1970s). Now there are six sizes, three of which (Churchill, Corona and Petit Corona) also come in elegant white tubes. A very limited number of Double Coronas were also produced in 2001. The cigars all have relatively similar girths, their ring gauges going from 42/16.67mm to 48/19.05mm. The richest in the range, and the clear favourites of many cigar connoisseurs, are the Serie A (there was also once a somewhat longer and fatter Serie B, discontinued in the 1970s) and the Regios (a *robusto*), but all the sizes are very good to excellent.

There is also a Saint Luis Rey brand made in Honduras by Altadis - see opposite. It was discontinued for a while, but was then re-launched, and now consists of eight sizes (including Churchill, Belicoso and Rothschild). These extremely good, flavourful and rather spicy cigars have Nicaraguan wrappers (Costa Rican for *maduro* versions), Nicaraguan binders and a filler blend from Honduras, Nicaragua and Peru. The Rothschild and Belicoso were rated an impressive 90 by *Cigar Insider,* and the Corona was given the same rating by *Cigar Aficianado* - highly respectable cigars by any standard.

Don't confuse Saint Luis Reys with the San Luis Rey brand - hand made in Cuba in very small quantities for the German market from the late 1980s to 2000 (in five sizes), or the German mass market machine mades produced by Villiger also called San Luis Rey. The Havanas have red and gold bands. The cigars made for Germany had black and gold bands. It is thought that they were produced to help to market the mass market cigars.

SAINT LUIS REY *Churchill*

HABANA, CUBA

CHURCHILLS: RING GAUGE 47 (18.65 mm), LENGTH 178 mm (7 inches)

SERIE A: RING GAUGE 46 (18.26 mm), LENGTH 143 mm (5⅝ inches)

REGIOS: RING GAUGE 48 (19.05 mm), LENGTH 127 mm (5 inches)

LONSDALES: RING GAUGE 42 (16.67 mm), LENGTH 166 mm (6½ inches)

CORONAS: RING GAUGE 42 (16.67 mm), LENGTH 139 mm (5½ inches)

Below is a Honduran Saint Luis Rey, the Rothschilde Maduro from the Reserva Especial range.

SAN CRISTOBAL

Launched in November 1999, San Christobal is the newest Havana brand, at the time of writing, one of the handful of what might be called post-boom brands (others include Cuaba and Vegas Robaina) - marketed and developed to maintain interest in Havanas, to cater for changing tastes, and to respond to competition from the Dominican Republic and elsewhere. The new brands (all of which have small ranges) have the additional advantage of being free from trademark problems, and are thus well positioned if the American embargo on Cuba is lifted. San Christobal de la Habana is the charming original name of Cuba's capital city.

Developed and produced by the La Corona factory, these are handsome, extremely good, rich, aromatic, mild to medium cigars - though they seemed to be much fuller flavoured when the brand first came on the market. They come in just four sizes, each of them named after one of the forts that defended Havana. Two of the sizes, La Fuerza, 141 mm (5 ½ inches) x 50 ring gauge/19.84 mm), a longer than usual *robusto*, and El Morro, 180mm (7 ⅛ inches) x 49 ring gauge/19.45mm), a thicker than normal Churchill, are entirely new and exclusive to the brand.

EL MORRO: RING GAUGE **49 (19.45 mm)**, LENGTH **180 mm (7⅛ inches)**

LA FUERZA: RING GAUGE **50 (19.84 mm)**, LENGTH **139 mm (5½ inches)**

LA PUNTA: RING GAUGE **52 (20.64 mm)**, LENGTH **139 mm (5½ inches)**

EL PRINCIPE: RING GAUGE **42 (16.67 mm)**, LENGTH **112 mm (4⅜ inches)**

SANCHO PANZA

Named after Don Quixote's servant in Miguel de Cervantes' novel, this is an old brand started in 1848 by German Emilio Olmstedt, who also founded El Rey del Mundo (see page 76). It was a minor marque, and went through various changes in ownership until it was acquired by the Rey del Mundo company in the 1930s. It then became better known, and very popular in Spain. Spain remained the main market after the Revolution, and it wasn't readily available elsewhere in the world until the 1990s. The cigars were rather milder than they are today: they are mild to medium flavoured, and good for daytime smoking. They don't tend to appeal to connoisseurs, who find them bland (apart from a slight saltiness), unless they are aged for some years. The quality of their construction has also been called into question from time to time. The largest cigars are unusually mild for their sizes - for Havanas.

Honduran Sancho Panzas have been on the market since 2001. They are fuller flavoured cigars than their Cuban counterparts, and of notable quality - with Connecticut Shade wrappers, Connecticut Broadleaf binders, and fillers of Honduran, Nicaraguan and Dominican Cuban seed (*piloto Cubano*) tobacco.

SANCHOS: RING GAUGE **47 (18.65 mm)**, LENGTH **235 mm (9¼ inches)**

CORONAS GIGANTES: RING GAUGE **47 (18.65 mm)**, LENGTH **178 mm (7 inches)**

BELICOSOS: RING GAUGE **52 (20.64 mm)**, LENGTH **139 mm (5½ inches)**

MOLINOS: RING GAUGE **42 (16.67 mm)**, LENGTH **166 mm (6½ inches)**

Officially launched in February 1998, in only one size, Trinidads were once the rarest of Havanas, shrouded in mystery. The brand is named after the Cuban south coast city of La Santissima Trinidad (The Holy Trinity), a UNESCO World Heritage Site. Production started at El Laguito in 1969. Trinidads were made in very small quantities, exclusively for the Cuban Council of State. From then on they became the Holy Grail for cigar enthusiasts, if only because they were virtually impossible to track down.

The brand's existence was originally confirmed by a journalist who visited the El Laguito factory, until then famous for its Cohibas, in 1992. But nobody knows exactly who was responsible for its origins. There were those who claimed it was Fidel Castro himself who suggested the cigars as exclusive gifts to foreign dignitaries when Cohibas became commercially available. But Castro more or less denied that it was him in an interview in 1994. The French magazine, *L'Amateur de Cigare* later reported that the Cuban Foreign Ministry was responsible.

In 1997, some of the diplomats who had received them decided to test their prices at auction. They were well rewarded when boxes of 25 Trinidads, sold first for £7,000 each and then, later in the year, for £10,000 each - or £400 a cigar. It was as a result of the extraordinary demand these sales implied that the Cubans decided to launch Trinidad to the public. A team at El Laguito was assembled by the factory Director, Emilia Tamayo, to prepare the brand for the market.

The Trinidads that eventually came on the market differed from those originally offered to the chosen few

CUBA **TRINIDAD** HABANA

TRINIDAD

before their public launch. Those (called Diplomats) were considered too earthy and heavy by some who smoked them. The one size, Fundadores (Founders), in which the brand came until 2003 was slightly fatter (with a 40/15.87mm ring guage rather than 38/14.9mm) than the original diplomatic cigar. The length remained 192mm (7 ½ inches), but the blend was changed to make it subtler, mellower, less harsh and less rich. The Cubans planned to launch a bigger range, eagerly awaited by cigar lovers, but took until November 2003 to do so. They then introduced three new sizes. The smallest is the Reyes 110 mm (4 ⅜ inches) x 40 ring gauge/ 15.87mm), next come the fragrant Coloniales - heavy girth Petit Coronas (44 ring gauge/17.2mm) - and finally come the Robusto Extra (an unusually long *robusto*). The cigars, launched in London, became available throughout the rest of the world (outside the United States, of course) only as recently as the beginning of 2004.

The tobacco for Trinidads comes from the same source as the leaves used to make Cohiba. That means they are the 'selection of the selection' from the five finest *vegas* (plantations) in the San Juan y Martinez and San Luis areas of the Vuelta Abajo region. However, although the leaves for Cohiba are fermented three times, those for Trinidad (like other major brands) are fermented twice. This means that Trinidads have a more approachable, medium flavour than their peers.

Nonetheless, Trinidads, good as they are, are very expensive and not for everyone. They come with gold bands simply printed with the brand name in black.

FUNDADORES: RING GAUGE 40 (15.87 MM), LENGTH 192 MM (7½ INCHES)

REYES: RING GAUGE 40 (15.87 MM), LENGTH 109 MM (4¼ INCHES)

COLONIALES: RING GAUGE 44 ((17.46 MM), LENGTH 129 MM (5⅛ INCHES)

ROBUSTO EXTRA: RING GAUGE 50 (19.84 MM), LENGTH 152 MM (6 INCHES)

BELOW, A DOMINICAN VERSION OF TRINIDAD (THE TRADEMARK WAS QUICKLY AND OPPORTUNISTICALLY REGISTERED) WITH EIGHT SIZES (INCLUDING FUNDADOR) HAS IDENTICAL BANDS AND LOGO TO THE CUBAN BRAND. THE CIGARS ARE MADE WITH ECUADORIAN SUMATRA WRAPPERS, CONNECTICUT BROADLEAF BINDERS, AND FILLER LEAVES FROM NICARAGUA, THE DOMINICAN REPUBLIC AND PERU. THEY ARE FULL-BODIED.

VEGAS ROBAINA

Launched in 1997, and originally only available in Spain, this brand is now more widely distributed. It is named after Don Alejandro Robaina, probably Cuba's most famous tobac-co grower - whose portrait appears on the box. He ran the family *vega* from 1950 in a tradition stretching back to 1845. One of the reasons for the quality the Robaina family's tobacco is that they still own their plantation, unlike most in Cuba, which are state-owned. The cigars are made in the H. Upmann factory. Vegas Robainas are robust (slightly harsh in some cases), very Cuban, and not for the novice or those who seek subtlety. The cigars are medium to full in flavour. At first, production difficulties caused a shortage of supplies, and one of the early problems was that rollers used to making other brands were switched to Robainas in an attempt to boost production, leading to a lack in consistency. But things seem to have been evened out. Try the Piramide-shaped Unicos or the Familiar (a *corona*). They are both full-bodied cigars, and notably spicy. The Don Alejandro is an equally good, spicy after-dinner cigar. The brand comes in five large sizes. A true impression of Vegas Robainas will only emerge once the cigars have had a chance to age further. The brand might well become one to be seriously reckoned with.

DON ALEJANDRO: RING GAUGE **49 (19.45 mm)**, LENGTH **194 mm (7⅝ inches)**

UNICOS: RING GAUGE **52 (20.64 mm)**, LENGTH **156 mm (6⅛ inches)**

FAMOSO: RING GAUGE **48 (19.05 mm)**, LENGTH **127 mm (5 inches)**

CLASICOS: RING GAUGE **42 (16.67 mm)**, LENGTH **166 mm (6½ inches)**

VEGUEROS

A new brand (launched internationally in 1998), it is named in honour of the vegueros (farmers) who grow Cuba's tobacco. Most unusually for an export quality, hand-made brand, it is made at the Francisco Donatien factory in the centre of the town of Pinar del Rio, in the heart of the Vuelta Abajo. The building, dating from 1868, was once a hospital, and then a prison. It became a cigar factory, catering for the domestic market, in 1961. The brand was originally created in the early 1990s to be sold to cigar-loving tourists who visited this region after Cuba started to build up its tourist trade in the wake of the collapse of the Soviet Union.

Because of its local success, it became an export brand, first sold in Germany, Switzerland and Canada. It was later available in South Africa and Britain, as well as other countries. There are only four sizes, three of which - the Mareva, Especial No. 1 and No. 2 - are similar to those found in the Montecristo range - though they are much cheaper and have a different flavour. Early export Vegueros, which are well made, were reported as being mild. The brand today is full-flavoured, rather rough, and lacks the finesse of the finest Havana cigars. Vegueros do, however, offer the Cuban experience at relatively low prices. And they look elegant with their dark wrappers and stylish green, white and gold bands.

MAREVA: RING GAUGE **42 (16.67 mm)**, LENGTH **129 mm (5⅛ inches)**

ESPECIALES No.1: RING GAUGE **38 (15.08 mm)**, LENGTH **192 mm (7½ inches)**

ESPECIALES No.2: RING GAUGE **38 (15.08 mm)**, LENGTH **152 mm (6 inches)**

SEONA: RING GAUGE **33 (13.10 mm)**, LENGTH **127 mm (5 inches)**

Non-Cuban cigar producers

ALTHOUGH, OVERALL, CUBA still produces the best hand-made cigars in the world, several other countries have been producing cigars of the highest quality over the last couple of decades.

Since the **Dominican Republic** is so close to Cuba, it has very good conditions for growing cigar tobacco. The main market for Dominican cigars is the world's biggest - the United States. Slow-burning *piloto Cubano* tobacco (grown from Cuban seed) with its full aroma, and *olor*, which burns well and is slightly sweet, are two of the best-known Dominican leaves. Imported tobacco is widely used for Dominican cigars, which are generally mild or medium flavoured.

ROLLER IN A CIGAR FACTORY IN LA PALMA, TENERIFE, ONE OF THE CANARY ISLANDS WHERE SOME QUALITY CIGARS ARE PRODUCED.

Honduras is almost as important a producer of hand-made cigars. Many Honduran cigars are made from filler tobacco grown from Cuban seed, and tend to be full-bodied. Shade-grown tobacco from Connecticut seed is also cultivated. But plenty of leaf from elsewhere is also used, wrappers in particular.

After the political upheavals and natural disasters of the last three decades, **Nicaragua** is now one of the world's major cigar exporters. Nicaragua's full-bodied filler leaf is often grown from Cuban seed. Nicaraguan wrappers can be pleasantly oily.

Dark, peppery **Mexican leaf** has been used for binders for some time, but now Mexican tobacco is also increasingly being used for wrappers, and to add sweetness and richness to filler blends of cigars made elsewhere. But the country, which has an old cigar tradition, also produces a number of fine hand-mades of its own. The best leaf comes from the San Andres Valley. Some of it is grown from Sumatra seed, introduced by Dutch cigar manufacturers in the 1950s.

Brazilian filler leaf - aromatic, sweet and a little peppery, though relatively mild - is now in demand for hand-made cigars. Brazilian binders and dark-brown wrappers (grown from Sumatra seed) are also used by some brands.

Costa Rica is starting to find a place in the cigar world as a producer of high-quality filler leaf. Ecuador has no cigar industry worth mentioning, but its excellent wrapper leaf (grown from Connecticut seed) is used on many brands made elsewhere. Peru has also started supplying interesting filler leaf.

The **United States** produces Connecticut Shade, some of the world's best and most expensive wrapper tobacco - normally used for mild and medium flavoured cigars. A different type of tobacco, Connecticut Broadleaf, is also used for

wrappers. Grown in the sun, it is very dark, slightly coarse, and used for cigars sold as *maduro*.

Further afield, **Indonesia** has become an important producer of high-quality wrappers (Jember in particular) for hand-mades. Shade grown tobacco (called TBN) is cultivated on Java. Indonesian filler (typically medium bodied and peppery) and binder leaf is also used for cigars made elsewhere.

The West African country of **Cameroon** has been an important source of wrapper leaf for some years. Cameroon wrappers, grown from Sumatra seed, are medium to dark brown and rich.

The **Canary Islands**, the Spanish possession off the Atlantic coast of North Africa, still produce premium cigars, though nothing like as much as in the 1960s and 70s, when a number of émigré Cuban cigar makers restarted manufacture there.

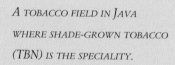

A TOBACCO FIELD IN JAVA WHERE SHADE-GROWN TOBACCO (TBN) IS THE SPECIALITY.

uente is one of the great names in the cigar-making world, with an enviable reputation for maintaining the highest standards. The history of the family encapsulates much of the history of cigar making outside Cuba since the beginning of the 20th century. Don Arturo Fuente, in common with many of his countrymen left Cuba in 1898 to go to Key West. After his first factory burned down, Don Arturo started production in Tampa, Florida, in 1912, making 'Clear Havanas' - the most expensive type of American cigar at the time, rolled from Cuban leaf. This, of course, was no longer possible after the American embargo on Cuba, and the Fuentes (by this time, Arturo's son Carlos was in charge) decided to set up production in Nicaragua - until the left-wing Sandanista revolution in the late 1970s made the production of high-quality cigars impossible. The family eventually moved to the Dominican Republic to start making cigars again. Arturo's grandchildren also entered the family business, which is now mainly based in Santiago, in the north of the Dominican Republic, in a huge (70,000 square foot) factory, opened in 1980. The family also has three other factories, and employs around 1800 people, 500 of whom are highly skilled rollers. The factories produce around 30 million cigars a year. The Fuentes work in cooperation with another very old tobacco family, the Newmans - who have been in the American cigar industry since 1895.

The Fuentes, who also produce other brands, have the distinction of first achieving what had previously been thought to be impossible: to produce high-quality wrapper leaves in the Dominican Republic. Despite experts claiming this wasn't possible because of the local soil and climate (until then, the best Dominican cigars had been dressed with leaf from Cameroon, Ecuador and Connecticut) they did so on their Chateau de la Fuente plantation near El Caribe. They soon established their success when one of the cigars wrapped in their new leaf topped *Cigar Aficionado's* tasting in autumn 1994, before it even went on sale. The Fuentes established another wrapper plantation in 1996.

ARTURO FUENTE

The standard range, one of the best-selling in the United States, is generally medium-bodied. It is made with dark brown Cameroon (or lighter Connecticut Shade) and Ecuadorian wrappers, and Dominican binders and fillers. The Chateau Fuente Royal Salute (193mm/7 ⅜ inches x 54 ring gauge/21.4mm), Canones (216 mm/8 ½ inches x 52 ring gauge/20.6mm and Double Chateau Fuente (6 ¼ inches x 50 ring gauge/19.8mm), are all big, smooth, flavourful, and very well-made cigars. The Chateau Fuente (a *robusto*), encased in cedar, is very good of its type. It is the same size as the Rothschild, which is also excellent. The Hemingway series consists of large, rich, spicy, figurados (the exemplary Masterpiece is 228mm/9 inches x 52 ring gauge/20.6mm) with sun-grown Ecuadorian or Connecticut wrappers and Dominican binders and fillers. Other top class cigars in the series are the Classic (178mm/7 inches x 48 ring gauge/19.05mm), the Signature (152mm/6 inches x 47 ring gauge/18.65mm) and the Short Story (102mm/4 inches x 45 ring gauge/17.86mm).

DON CARLOS: RING GAUGE 52 (20,64 MM), LENGTH 136 MM (5 ⅜ INCHES)

SEL SUP 4: RING GAUGE 43 (17,07 MM), LENGTH 127 MM (5 INCHES)

TORPEDPO NO. IV: RING GAUGE 50 (19,84 MM), LENGTH 120 MM (4 3/4 INCHES)

OPUS X: RING GAUGE 48 (19,05 MM), LENGTH 158 MM (6 ¼ INCHES)

THE RICH, ELEGANT ARTURO FUENTE OPUS X SERIES (WITH MUCH BIGGER AND MORE ORNATE BANDS THAN OTHER FUENTE CIGARS) WAS LAUNCHED IN 1995 AS THE FLAGSHIP BRAND, WRAPPED IN THE FAMILY'S OWN LOCALLY-GROWN LEAF. THE SERIES, PARTICULARLY THE MASSIVE RESERVA A (235 MM/9 ¼ INCHES), THE TORPEDO SHAPED RESERVA NO. 2 AND THE IMPRESSIVE ROBUSTO, IMMEDIATELY HIT THE SPOT WITH SERIOUS CIGAR LOVERS, BUT VERY LIMITED PRODUCTION HAS MADE IT HARD FOR FANS TO GET HOLD OF THESE CIGARS.

ASHTON

$\mathcal{F}$ounded by Philidelphia tobacconist Robert Levin in 1985, this is a high-quality brand which has established itself as a favourite with many who like mild to medium cigars. There are five lines, all manufactured by the Fuente family in the Dominican Republic. The standard ('Classic') selection consists of 14 medium-flavoured sizes with Connecticut shade wrappers and Dominican binders and filler leaf.

The Cabinet Selection of cigars, introduced in 1988, are aged for a year. They are somewhat smoother than the main range (there are eight sizes) with as many as six tobaccos used for the line as a whole. With Connecticut Shade wrappers, these mild, aromatic cigars, are all *figurados* and have more ornate bands than the simple white and yellow of the basic line.

The Aged Maduro line (seven sizes) is dark and sweet, and uses Connecticut broadleaf (rather than shade) wrappers. The full-bodied, highly flavourful, and very well constructed Ashton VSG (Virgin Sun Grown) series, with its Ecuadorian wrappers came on to the market in 1999, and was an immediate success. In November 2003, Ashton introduced five sizes of the Heritage Puro Sol line. This was an even bigger success, gaining a 90 rating from *Cigar Insider*. It is the only Ashton line to carry sun-grown Cameroon wrappers. The Magnum (*robusto*) and Double Robusto (a longer than normal *robusto*) sizes of the standard line are recommended as a good mild to medium, but aromatic smoke.

SPELLBOUND: RING GAUGE 50 (19.84 mm), LENGTH 192 mm (5¼ inches)

SORCERER: RING GAUGE 49 (19.45 mm), LENGTH 178 mm (7 inches)

ROBUSTO: RING GAUGE 50 (19.84 mm), LENGTH 139 mm (5½ inches)

CORONA GORDA: RING GAUGE 46 (18.26 mm), LENGTH 145 mm (5¾ inches)

AVO

*B*eirut-born Avo Uvezian is a musician and composer who trained at the famous Julliard School of Music and was personal pianist to the Shah of Iran. He then moved to the United States to play jazz. He was a great lover of cigars and later teamed up with Hendrik Kelner (who produces Davidoff cigars) to launch his own brand in New York in 1988. Davidoff distributed Avo cigars from 1995, and its parent company, Oettinger, bought the brand in 1998.

Uvezian and Kelner both understand the importance of careful composition, and all Avo cigars are well constructed. Both his not especially cheap standard line of 13 cigars and the seven more expensive and richer cigars in the more recent XO Trio and Quartetto series carry high-quality Connecticut Shade wrappers, Cuban seed binders, and Dominican *piloto Cubano* fillers from the Cibao valley. They get fuller-flavoured as the cigars get bigger, and range from medium to full in strength. The XO Intermezzo (a *robusto*), Maestoso and Notturno are particularly successful. The Domaine series of *figurados* (with filler from Uvezian's own plantation) has dark Ecuadorian wrappers. A limited edition cigar (178mm/7 inches x 50 ring gauge/20mm) made with sun-grown Ecuador wrappers was produced for Avo Uvezian's 75th birthday in 2001, and another (a *corona* extra with a pointed head), with full-flavoured Dominican *piloto Cubano* filler, for his 78th birthday in March 2004. This is a distinguished brand by any standards.

MAESTRO: RING GAUGE 48 (19.05 mm), LENGTH 178 mm (7 inches)

PRELUDIO: RING GAUGE 40 (15.87 mm), LENGTH 152 mm (6 inches)

PRELUDIO TUBOS: RING GAUGE 40 (15.87 mm), LENGTH 152 mm (6 inches)

INTERMEZZO: RING GAUGE 50 (19.84 mm), LENGTH 139 mm (5½ inches)

BALMORAL

The Netherlands is one of the world's most important producers of machine-made cigars, normally using tobacco from Sumatra (Indonesia was once a Dutch colony), Brazil and sometimes Cuba. The industry started in about 1830 in Amsterdam, with many hand-made brands to satisfy the local market until the Second World War. Today, only a couple are produced. But with such a long tradition, it isn't surprising that the Dutch firm of Agio, one of Europe's biggest cigar manufacturers, decided to launch a new brand of long filler hand-mades. Balmorals, whose bands carry an image of the British Royal family's castle in Scotland, are made in the town of San Pedro de Macoris in the Dominican Republic, with Dominican and Brazilian fillers, Dominican binders and Ecuadorian shade grown wrappers. The name itself has been carried by Dutch cigars for more than a century, and there is a machine-made Balmoral brand, also made by Agio, available in Europe. So don't confuse the two. The Royal Selection, as it is called, consists of six sizes of well-made mild to medium cigars. *Maduro* versions of the brand (with different coloured bands) have dark Brazilian wrappers.

BALMORAL: RING GAUGE **42 (16.67 mm)**, LENGTH **149 mm (5⅞ inches)**

BAUZA

This brand, introduced in 1980, is made by Tabacalera Fuente (owned by the famous Fuente family, who also make their own cigars) in the Dominican Republic. They are well-made, high-quality, aromatic, mostly medium-bodied cigars, and are named after an old Cuban domestic brand. They are sold at competitive prices. The rich, oily wrappers come from Ecuador, the binders from the Dominican Republic and the filler blend is composed of leaves from Nicaragua and the Dominican Republic. There are eight sizes, almost all of which are very good. Try the Grecos (140mm/5 ½ inches x 42 ring gauge/16.67mm); the spicy, medium to full-bodied Jaguar (6 ½ inches x 42/16.67mm), and the Casa Grande (172mm/6 ¾ inches x 48/19mm). The Robusto is surprisingly good and full of flavour.

CASA GRANDE: RING GAUGE **48 (19.05 mm)**, LENGTH **171 mm (6⁷⁄₁₀ inches)**

CAO

CAO cigars (the initials are those of the founder, Cano A. Ozgener) have created a reputation for themselves since they came on to the market in 1995 with the Black Label range, made in Honduras. The line was discontinued, but reappeared in 2002. Smooth medium-bodied cigars, made in limited quantities, they come in cedar sleeves and hand-painted boxes. Wrappers are shade grown Ecuadorian Connecticut, and filler tobaccos come from Nicaragua, Honduras and Mexico.

The CAO Gold line, launched in 1996, was soon in great demand. The Double Corona received a 90 rating in the October 1998 issue of *Cigar Aficionado*. The six medium-bodied sizes are made in Nicaragua with Connecticut seed Ecuadorian wrappers, and Nicaraguan binders and fillers.

In 1998, CAO launched the L'Anniversaire line to celebrate the company's 30th anniversary. These were originally *maduro* cigars made in Costa Rica in four sizes with Connecticut Broadleaf wrappers, Sumatran seed, Ecuadorian binders and Dominican and Nicaraguan fillers. They are medium to full bodied. There are now also very highly rated L'Anniversaire cigars with Cameroon wrappers made in Nicaragua (which also supplies the fillers and binders). L'Anniversaire eXtreme (with a Nicaraguan filler blend, using two types of *ligero*) are very full-bodied. Other CAO lines include: the full-bodied Criollo (with Cuban seed Nicaraguan filler), and the Brazilia range - fat cigars with Brazilian wrappers.

PATO: RING GAUGE 50 (19.84 mm), LENGTH 124 mm (4⁷⁄₈ inches)

PAMPA: RING GAUGE 40 (15.59 mm), LENGTH 102 mm (4 inches)

BOMBA: RING GAUGE 50 (19.84 mm), LENGTH 152 mm (6 inches)

CASA BLANCA

The name means White House, and Casa Blancas were first produced for the Republican National Convention, and smoked at President Ronald Reagan's inauguration dinner at the White House in 1981. The brand's speciality is cigars with huge ring gauges (although there are also two or three more modest sizes). If you want a seriously big cigar, look no further than the Magnum with its 60 ring gauge (23.81mm), and the Jeroboam and Half Jeroboam, both with massive 66 ring gauges (26.19mm), the former weighing in at 254 mm (10 inches).

Even though these big cigars are essentially oddities, they have their fans, and are popular in the United States. They must be: over 1 ½ million Casa Blancas are produced every year at Santiago in the Dominican Republic. But they don't really appeal to the serious connoisseur looking for a complex smoke. Nonetheless these mild and smooth cigars (with a flavour which used to be typical of Dominicans) are well made.

Casa Blancas come in light (*claro*) Connecticut wrappers, with some sizes also available in dark *maduro*, with Connecticut Broadleaf wrappers. The filler leaves come from the Dominican Republic and Brazil, and binders are Mexican.

If you don't simply want to fill your mouth, try the more conventionally-sized Lonsdale, which is a very good, very mild smoke which burns and draws easily, as does the Corona. These sizes are good for beginners.

MAGNUM: RING GAUGE **60 (23,81 mm)**, LENGTH **178 mm (7 inches)**

LONSDALE: RING GAUGE **42 (16,67 mm)**, LENGTH **166 mm (6½ inches)**

CUESTA REY

*T*his is a very old brand, founded in Tampa, Florida, in 1884 by Angel La Madrid Cuesta and Peregrino Rey, to make 'Clear Havana' cigars for the American market from Cuban tobacco. The firm was taken over by another old Tampa business, M&N, owned by the Newman family, a major name in the American cigar industry, in 1958. The cigars were originally made in the United States. Production in the Dominican Republic began in the 1980s, and was put in the hands of the Fuente family. The Cabinet Selection range started in 1958 with just one size, the No. 95. It was one of the first premium cigars to use Cameroon wrappers. As a result of its success, Stanford Newman quickly added three more sizes: the 8-9-8, the No. 1 and No.2. Then, in 1986, with the help of the Fuentes, the No.1884, the first new size for more than 20 years, was added. It was the first Cabinet Selection cigar to come with a Connecticut Shade wrapper. In 1999, the No.47 was added to the range, and is available in Cameroon or Connecticut Broadleaf wrappers. These are all well-made mild cigars. The Cuesta-Rey Centenario (Centennial) Collection is a big range of aged medium-bodied smooth and creamy cigars available in both Connecticut Shade and Connecticut Broadleaf (*maduro*) wrappers. They are also made in the Domincan Republic. The No. 7 is a very good *robusto*.

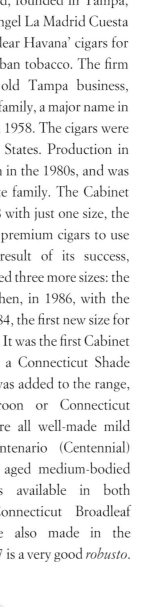

PYRAMIDE: RING GAUGE 52 (20.64 mm), LENGTH 192 mm (5¼ inches)

ROBUSTO No.7: RING GAUGE 50 (19.84 mm), LENGTH 114 mm (4½ inches)

CAPTIVA TUBOS: RING GAUGE 42 (16.67 mm), LENGTH 127 mm (5 inches)

The name of Davidoff has been virtually synonymous with cigars, and cigar shops, for many decades. In recent years, the brand has also given its name to a vast range of high quality smokers' accessories - as well as numerous luxury products, including clothing, well beyond smoking and cigars.

Davidoff cigars were, of course, originally made in Cuba, starting in the 1940s with the Chateau series, produced at the Hoyo de Monterrey factory. Then, in 1969, Zino Davidoff was accorded the honour of having a Havana brand, with its distinctive, elegant white and gold bands, named after him. Some sizes were made at the El Laguito factory, later famous for making the Cohiba brand, others continued to be made at the Hoyo factory. Cuban Davidoffs, sold at premium prices (more expensive than other Havanas) quickly became fashionable, and held the position that Cohibas have today in the pecking order of Havana cigars.

In 1970, Zino Davidoff went into partnership with Ernst Schneider's Swiss firm, Oettinger (based in Basle) one of Europe's biggest cigar importers. It was Schneider who saw the potential in the brand, helping to develop the Havana line. He also set-up a chain of Davidoff shops around the world - to add to the one that Zino himself had opened on Geneva's Rue de Rive before the Second World War. There are now 50 shops bearing the name, the latest (at the time of writing) in Dusseldorf.

Cuban Davidoffs came in three ranges, each with a different flavour. The Chateau series was the fullest, although no more than medium. Next came the Thousand series; the lightest were the very mild Dom

DAVIDOFF

Perignons consisting of a Churchill (introduced in 1977); the No. 1; the No.2 (both with twisted caps); and the Ambassadrice. All these cigars, as well as the 80th Aniversario special edition to mark Zino Davidoff's 80th birthday in 1986, are now sought-after collectors' items, and fetch very high prices.

A dispute arose between the Cuban state monopoly, Cubatabaco, and Davidoff in the late 1980s. Nobody is quite sure whether it was about quality (as was claimed) or the fact that Cohiba was being positioned as the leading Havana brand. In the year 1990 Oettinger announced that there would be no further production in Cuba (although export of Havana Davidoffs continued until late 1992). From then on, Davidoff cigars were made at Santiago, in the Dominican Republic, under the supervision of Hendrik Kelner. Zino Davidoff himself died in 1994, aged 88, but the brand continues as among the Dominican Republic's best known, best made, and most expensive cigars. They have by no means the same taste as the Cuban brand, but keep many of the same names, and the same bands. That the brand has remained prestigious is a remarkable achievement.

Dominican Davidoffs are generally mild to medium in flavour, excellent for daytime smoking, and are made with superb Connecticut Shade wrappers and Dominican filler leaf. The brand consists of a large number of sizes in five regular ranges. A new, and very successful, line of substantially fuller Davidoffs, of very high quality, were produced for the Millennium. There are also small machine-made Davidoffs produced in Europe, and sold in cartons: they are Davidoffs in name only.

The basic line (No.1, No. 2, No.3, Tubos and Ambassadrice) is notably mild, as is the very smooth Aniversario series (obviously not to be confused with the Cuban special editon), made with tobacco matured for up to four years. Even the large Aniversarios No 1 and No 2, are remarkably mild for their size, but the No. 3 is richer and more aromatic. The Thousand (Mille) series veers towards medium (the spicy 4000 is particularly recommended).

Special C I Culebra: ring gauge 33 (15.09 mm), length 165 mm (6½ inches)

Special blend, Special B: ring gauge 41 (16.27 mm), length 139 mm (5½ inches)

Special blend, Special T: ring gauge 52 (20.64 mm), length 152 mm (6 inches)

Special blend, Special R : ring gauge 50 (19.84 mm), length 123 mm (4⅞ inches)

Special blend, Double R: ring gauge 50 (19.84 mm), length 192 mm (7½ inches)

Full blend, grand Cru No. 1: ring gauge 43 (17.07 mm), length 155 mm (6⅛ inches)

The Grand Cru series is altogether richer. The Special series, mainly figurados with big girths, is also fuller bodied, and richer, and has wrappers which are darker than the rest of the range. The Special R is a complex robusto, and the Special T (a piramide) is also a connoisseur's cigar of the highest quality.

Full blend, Grand Cru No. 2: ring gauge 43 (17.07 mm), length 127 mm (5 inches)

Full blend, Grnad Cru No. 3: ring gauge 43 (17.07 mm), length 127 mm (5 inches)

Full blend, Grand Cru No. 4: ring gauge 41 (16.27 mm), length 127 mm (5 inches)

Full blend, Grand Cru No. 5: ring gauge 41 (16.27 mm), length 102 mm (4 inches)

Anniversario blend, No. 1 Tubos: ring gauge 48 (19.05 mm), length 127 mm (8 inches)

Anniversario blend, No 2: ring gauge 48 (19.05 mm), length 178 mm (7 inches)

MILLENIUM BLEND, LONSDALE : RING GAUGE 43 (17.07 mm), LENGTH 152 mm (6 inches)

MILLENIUM BLEND, CHURCHILL: RING GAUGE 48 (19.05 mm), LENGTH 170 mm (6¾ inches)

MILLENIUM BLEND, ROBUSTO: RING GAUGE 50 (19.84 mm), LENGTH 132 mm (5¼ inches)

MILD BLEND, No. 1: RING GAUGE 38 (15.08 mm), LENGTH 192 mm (7½ inches)

MILD BLEND, No. 2: RING GAUGE 38 (15.08 mm), LENGTH 152 mm (6 inches)

MILD BLEND, No. 3: RING GAUGE 30 (11.91 mm), LENGTH 129 mm (5⅛ inches)

MILD BLEND, AMBASSADRICE: RING GAUGE 26 (10.32 mm), LENGTH115 mm (4 ⅜ inches)

THE DOUBLE R IS A DOUBLE CORONA MUCH APPRECIATED BY AFICIONADOS. LIMITED EDITION CIGARS (MADE WITH TOBACCO ONLY FROM THE NOTABLE 2000 HARVEST), WITH ECUADORIAN WRAPPER LEAVES CAME ON TO THE MARKET IN 2003. THE FIRST DAVIDOFF 'VINTAGE' CIGARS, THEY WERE MADE IN A PANATELA EXTRA SIZE.

DON DIEGO

Now made by Altadis, at La Romana in the Dominican Republic, this brand was originally developed by Pepe Garcia of the famous Cuban cigar family, then in exile, in the Canary Islands from the 1960s until the mid-1970s. The Canary Island cigars had very different characteristics to the Dominican versions. These are aromatic mild to medium cigars with a first-rate construction, good for daytime smoking.

The smooth basic line, with its simple bands, comes with fine Connecticut Shade wrappers, Dominican binders and a filler blend from the Dominican Republic and Brazil. There are 12 sizes, two of them tubed. The Grande, Torpedo and Robusto are recommended.

The fuller-flavoured Reserve line has more elaborate bands and comes in ten sizes (including *maduro* versions). The wrappers used are Ecudorian Connecticut Shade, binders Dominican, and the filler blend is from the Dominican Republic and Brazil. The *maduros* have Connecticut Broadleaf wrappers, Nicaraguan binders and fillers from the Dominican Republic, Peru and Nicaragua. The line is unusual in carrying both a 178mm/7 inch Belicoso and an impressive 127mm/5 inch Petite Belicoso - perfect after lunch.

The Aniversario line was created to celebrate the brand's 40th anniversary. There are six sizes with Ecuadorian shade-grown wrappers, Connecticut Broadleaf binders, and a Dominican/Peruvian/ Nicaraguan filler blend. The Lord Rothchilde [sic] gained a 91 rating in the November 2003 issue of *Cigar Insider*, and the No.2 (a Belicoso) got 90. Don Diego also lends its name to the Playboy and Players Club series.

ROBUSTO: RING GAUGE **50 (19.84 MM)**, LENGTH **127 MM (5 INCHES)**

TORPEDO NATURAL: RING GAUGE **50 (19.84 MM)**, LENGTH **152 MM (6 INCHES)**

DON RAMOS

*T*his is a well-made brand made in the village of Cofradia, on the banks of the Joyoa river, close to the Caribbean coast of Honduras. Honduran cigars, often made from Cuban seed tobacco, are characteristically full-bodied, but Don Ramos is relatively light. The range of around ten sizes comes in medium to large ring gauges. They are mellow, spicy,

medium-bodied cigars with Dominican and Honduran filler leaf. The bundles are numbered but the boxes, and one or two of the tubes have names. Production started under the supervision of Frank Llaneza of Villazon (acquired by General Cigar in 1997), primarily designed for the British market, where they were first introduced in 1982.

CHURCHILL, TUBOS: RING GAUGE **47** (18,65 mm), LENGTH **170 mm** (6¾ inches)

DON TOMAS

*P*art of General Cigar's portfolio since 2004, this well-made Honduran brand was developed in 1973, and is made in the Talanga Valley on a 1,300 acre estate. It is available in three lines - all differently priced. The medium-strength standard series comes in dark Indonesian wrappers (with Colombian binders and fillers from the Dominican Republic, Mexico and Nicaragua) in a big range, including a 'Corona' with an unusually large ring gauge of 50/19.84mm. The International series consists of only four numbered premium-priced sizes

made with rich Cuban seed Honduran tobacco. Special Edition has five very aromatic medium to full bodied super-premium priced sizes with Connecticut Shade wrappers, Mexican binders, and filler from the Dominican Republic, Mexico and Nicaragua. The brand also has other lines, including Corojo cigars which come in tissue paper, and are made with Cuban seed wrappers and Mexican binders and fillers; and a limited edition of four aged *figurados* with Cameroon wrappers and fillers from the Dominican Republic, Brazil and Mexico.

CETROS: RING GAUGE **44** (17.46 mm), LENGTH **166 mm** (6½ inches)

BELICOSO: RING GAUGE **52** (20,64 mm), LENGTH **152 mm** (6 inches)

unhill is one the best-known names in the world of tobacco and fine cigars, and has been since its original London tobacco shop was opened by Alfred Dunhill in 1907, followed by others in New York and Paris. Alfred Dunhill was one of the first cigar retailers to understand the importance of having a walk-in humidor. Later, the firm was instrumental in the success of Montecristo. Dunhill had its own Havana brand of mild cigars from 1984 to 1989, originally, and misguidedly, designed to compete with Davidoff. Beautifully packaged, they had elegant red bands, featuring the elongated letter 'd'.

DUNHILL

Collectors are prepared to pay very high prices for these.

Before the Cuban Dunhill brand was created, a number of Havana brands, exclusive to Dunhill (as the original Chateau series had been to Davidoff) had also been on the market. They were called Don Candido, Flor del Punto and Don Alfredo, and were discontinued in 1982, when the deal to make Cuban Dunhills was signed.

After the agreement with the Cubans came to an end (interestingly, around the same time as Davidoff fell out with Cubatabaco), production of Dunhill's flagship cigars moved to La Romana in the Dominican Republic, and are now made by Altadis. These are Dunhill's Aged Cigars. There are 13 sizes, each made with Dominican (*piloto Cubano* and *Olor*) and Brazilian fillers, wrapped in Connecticut Shade leaf. Aged for a minimum of three months before they are distributed, they have stylish blue, white and gold bands (the Dunhill logo was changed to its present script, from a more modern design, in 1995). They are well made and blended, burn evenly and have a delicate aroma, and a mild to medium flavour, without being too

rich. The Peravias, Altimiras and the torpedo shaped Centenas are particularly elegant smokes. Vintages have been declared for Dominican Dunhills because they are made with leaf from only one year's harvest (the 'vintage' is the year of the harvest, not the year of manufacture).

Dunhill's Honduran Selection, launched in 1998, is fuller, and consists of five sizes with green, white and gold bands. They are blended with filler leaf from the Dominican Republic, Mexico and Brazil, with binders from Mexico, and wrappers from Indonesia: a complex blend designed to give a balanced medium smoke with a spicy finish. They are cigars very much for the experienced smoker seeking a fuller flavour. Try the Toro, a long *robusto*.

Dunhill also has a range made on the Canary Islands, perhaps the best-known cigars currently being produced there. These come in a range of just five sizes. Distinguished by their brownish, white and gold bands (they used to be black, white and gold), they offer a mild to medium flavour with a touch of sweetness. Although well constructed, they make a rather less polished smoke than other Dunhills. Canary Island Dunhills are only available in the United States.

There is also a machine-made Dunhill line. At one point a range of Montecruz cigars (milder than normal) was also exclusively made for Dunhill in the Dominican Republic.

Today, the Dunhill brand name extends to clothing, fragrances and accessories (including lighters and humidors), as well as tobacco products. There are many Dunhill shops around the world, but several of those in the United States closed recently. The cigarette and cigar side of the brand is owned by British American Tobacco.

The new Dunhill signed range was launched at the end of 2001 in Britain, and later in other countries. The cigars carry red bands, and each box is numbered and literally signed by many of the people responsible for making and checking the cigars. Made at the small Cuevas & Torino factory in Navarette in the Dominican Republic, they are fuller flavoured and more tightly constructed than the Aged line. There are six sizes, with large ring gauges, including unusually fat Churchills and Robustos, and a Torpedo.

CABRERA: RING GAUGE **48** (19.05 mm), LENGTH **178 mm** (7 inches)

VALVERDE: RING GAUGE **42** (16.67 mm), LENGTH **139 mm** (5½ inches)

ALTAMIRA: RING GAUGE **48** (19.05 mm), LENGTH **127 mm** (5 inches)

ROMANA: RING GAUGE **50** (19.84 mm), LENGTH **115 mm** (4½ inches)

CHURCHILL: RING GAUGE **50** (19.84 mm), LENGTH **178 mm** (7 inches)

TORPEDO: RING GAUGE **50** (19.84 mm), LENGTH **152 mm** (6 inches)

EL CREDITO

La Gloria Cubana is one of the most popular premium brands in the United States. It wasn't available elsewhere due to trademark problems (there is a Havana brand of the same name). But, now that the brand has been taken over by General Cigar, they are sold internationally - as El Creditos.

So the history of the El Credito (officially launched in May 2002) is the history of the non-Havana La Gloria Cubana, founded in 1972 in Miami by Ernesto Carrillo, and originally only sold locally. The Carillo family had been in the cigar business since 1907, and once owned the El Credito factory in Havana. Hence the name, and the fact that the label on El Credito boxes is based on the lithograph once used for Cuban El Creditos.

Production of La Gloria Cubanas was mostly moved to the Dominican Republic in 1995. These very attractive, reasonably-priced cigars are medium to full-bodied, with dark Sumatra wrappers from Ecuador (Connecticut Broadleaf in the case of the sweetish *maduros*), binders from Nicaragua, and fillers blended from leaves from the Dominican Republic and leaves from Nicaragua.

La Gloria Cubanas come in 23 sizes, but El Creditos come in only seven (not all of which are available in some countries). The larger ones are the best: try the Robusto (the La Gloria version is called Wavell) or the Churchill, if you like rich cigars. Limited edition Gold Reserve El Creditos are wrapped in gold paper, each box signed by their founder Ernesto Carillo.

CHURCHILL MADURO: RING GAUGE **50** (19.84 mm), LENGTH **178 mm** (7 inches)

CRISTAL DELUXE NATURAL: RING GAUGE **46** (16.67 mm), LENGTH **139 mm** (5¾ inches)

EXQUISITOS MADURO: RING GAUGE **40** (15.59 mm), LENGTH **115 mm** (4½ inches)

TORPEDO NATURAL: RING GAUGE **54** (22 mm), LENGTH **152 mm** (6 inches)

FLOR DE COPAN

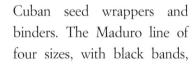

Cigar production in Honduras is centred in three areas: Danli, on the border with Nicaragua to the south; San Pedro Sula, close to the Caribbean coast, and Santa Rosa de Copan, near Guatemala to the north, where the Flor de Copan cigars are made. The brand, owned by Altadis, was re-introduced in 1999. The standard line comes in eight sizes made entirely with Honduran tobacco, and Cuban seed wrappers and binders. The Maduro line of four sizes, with black bands, was introduced in 2001, and has wrappers from Costa Rica. The two lines have different sizes, apart from the Robusto/Rothschild. Several of the sizes, including the *figurado* Belicosos of the standard line come in elegant cedar wrapping. The brand is very traditionally Honduran: gutsy and aimed at robust smokers.

ROBUSTO: RING GAUGE **50 (19,84 mm)**, LENGTH **127 mm (5 inches)**

GRIFFIN'S

This brand of extremely well-constructed mild to medium cigars was founded by Bernard Grobet, an associate of Zino Davidoff and owner of a Geneva nightclub after which the cigars are named. Grobet was one of the first Europeans to start production in the Dominican Republic. The cigars were created, under the supervision of Hendrik Kelner, at Tobacos Dominicanos in Santiago. Now the brand is owned by Oettinger The basic line of these subtle and superior cigars has pale Connecticut Shade

Fuerte

wrappers and Dominican fillers, ideal for daytime or occasional smoking. The brand is widely distributed, particularly in Davidoff shops. They are aimed at the higher end of the market. There are over a dozen sizes, five of them numbered. The long Prestige (152mm/8 inches), the medium flavoured No.300 and Robusto, and the slim Privilege are the highlights of the range. Some sizes come with *maduro* (Connecticut Broadleaf) wrappers. The Griffin's Fuerte line, carrying an additional red band, is fuller and spicier.

100: RING GAUGE **38 (15.08 mm)**, LENGTH **178 mm (7 inches)**

PRESTIGE : RING GAUGE **50 (19,84 mm)**, LENGTH **192 mm (7½ inches)**

The Henry Clay brand is included in this directory not particularly for its quality, although it has its devotees, but because of its long and distinguished history. It is surprising that Altadis, which now owns it, hasn't developed and marketed the brand more vigorously to exploit its heritage.

Henry Clay was originally a famous early Havana brand, dating back to the middle of the 19th century, and was then called La Flor de Henry Clay. It was named after the celebrated 19th Century American statesman, senator and presidential candidate, who died in 1852, and was so fond of cigars that he used to hand them out to fellow members of the Senate. See pages 191. It is possible that he had business interests, like other Americans of his time, in Cuba, and this might explain why his name was chosen for the brand. Although many American politicians and presidents have been cigar lovers, he is the only one to have a brand named after him.

The brand was once owned by Gustavo Bock, one of the great names in cigar history, and the box labels carried his signature. The notorious tobacco magnate James B ('Buck') Duke (see pages 28-29), and his American Tobacco Company managed to gain control 90 per cent of Cuban cigar exports by 1902, through a series of companies known as the Trust. The brands the Trust took over included Henry Clay (though it was still overseen by Bock at the time). Duke's plan was to streamline manufacture and guarantee leaf supplies. It met with considerable local opposition, not least from his labour force, with whom he never had good relations.

HENRY CLAY

Eventually, as a result of these industrial problems, most of the Trust's brands, including Henry Clay, moved to Trenton, New Jersey, in 1932. The cigars were still made with Cuban tobacco. The brand eventually became part of the Consolidated Cigar Corporation's portfolio, and later that of Altadis in the late 1990s. Today, Henry Clay boxes still carry an illustration of the original Cuban factory on the inside of their lids.

Henry Clays have been made in the Dominican Republic for several years. There have been several changes to the range and the blend over the last couple of decades. There were only three sizes by the mid-1990s: Breva Fina, Breva Conserva, and Breva, all medium to full-bodied, with mid-Brown Connecticut broadleaf wrappers. Then Consolidated Cigar added six new even fuller bodied sizes with dark Cuban-seed wrappers from Nicaragua. They included the Cedro Deluxe, wrapped in cedar; the torpedo-shaped Obelix; and Fantasias, which came in glass tubes. The blend, and the basic range, was changed again in 1999 and a successful line with Habana 2000 wrappers was later launched, of which the Robusto and Mirabelle attracted praise from critics. (Habana 2000 is a Cuban seed hybrid). Now there are seven sizes of Henry Clay, all maduros, with Connecticut Broadleaf wrappers and Dominican fillers and binders.

Henry Clays are strong and aromatic, not for those who seek for complexity. The Toro (at 152mm/6 inches) is essentially a long *robusto*; the Rothchilde is a more conventionally sized one. The cigars are well, but not brilliantly, constructed.

BREVA FINA: RING GAUGE **48 (19,05 mm)**, LENGTH **166 mm (6½ inches)**

BREVA CONSERVA: RING GAUGE **46 (18,26 mm)**, LENGTH **143 mm (5⅝ inches)**

BREVA: RING GAUGE **42 (16,67 mm)**, LENGTH **139 mm (5½ inches)**

NAMED AFTER ONE OF AMERICA'S MOST POPULAR STATESMEN, HENRY CLAY IS ONE OF THE OLDEST ORIGINAL HAVANA BRANDS, QUOTED IN A POEM ENTITLED 'THE BETROTHED' PENNED IN 1898 BY RUDYARD KIPLING (THERE'S CALM IN A HENRY CLAY). FOLLOWING THE SAME DESIGN AS THE FIRST HAVANA HENRY CLAY, THE ORIGINAL JULIAN ALVAREZ FACTORY IS STILL FEATURED ON THE BOX. HENRY CLAY CIGARS WERE AMONG THE FIRST IN THE WORLD TO FEATURE THE HABANA 2000 WRAPPER.

The Excalibur series is among the very best non-Havana medium to full-bodied cigars on the market: rich and slow burning. They are technically part of the Honduran Hoyo de Monterrey brand and are also briefly discussed on page 78. I give them a full entry here not only because of their quality, but also because they are among the most popular non-Cubans on the market in both the United States and Europe. They appeal to connoisseurs.

Now made by General Cigar, the line was created in 1977, the brainchild of Villazon's Frank Llaneza, one of the greatest names in the cigar world, and the hugely knowledgeable and influential Lew Rothman, owner of the American company, J.R. Tobacco. The name comes from the sword given to King Arthur by the Lady in the Lake, in the legend of Camelot and the Knights of the Round Table. Today, production is under the supervision of Estelo Padron, the renowned Honduran cigar master. That's quite a pedigree.

HOYO DE MONTERREY EXCALIBUR

Excaliburs are particularly special because they are exceptionally well-balanced, and more medium-bodied than typical Honduran cigars. Their consistent quality and exemplary construction is another attraction for aficionados and is reflected in their price. Their packaging, which was recently revamped, also adds to the style and prestige of the brand.

The cigars in the basic line come with either Connecticut Shade wrappers or, for *maduros*, Connecticut Broadleaf.

The 'natural' Connecticut Shade cigars come with Broadleaf binders. The precise filler blend varies from cigar to cigar, but is mainly Honduran and Nicaraguan, with Cuban seed Dominican leaves also used for some sizes. Excaliburs have a complex, slightly nutty flavour, a smooth, well-rounded, creamy smoke.

The 1066 series, added to the brand in the last few years, is also medium to full-bodied and, with dark Cameroon wrappers, is designed to be richer and to appeal to those with a taste for Cuban cigars. The name is derived from the date of the Battle of Hastings - nothing to do with Arthurian legend, but the date when the Normans, under William the Conqueror, invaded Britain. The names of the cigars (which come in five sizes) are, confusingly, those of characters in the story of Camelot. They include Galahad, Lancelot and Merlin. All these cigars have big ring gauges (45/17.7mm to 54/21.3mm). One of the most interesting in the series is the punchy Dark Knight (146mm/5 ¾ inches x 54/21.3mm), introduced in 2003, and the strongest of the brand. The wrapper might look like a standard Connecticut Broadleaf *maduro*, but is in fact made with Havana seed Connecticut leaf. This leaf, commonly used in the United States until 1833, was eventually replaced by broadleaf, but is now being used again for some brands. The leaves are smoother and oilier than broadleaf tobacco, and fuller in flavour.

Churchill tubos: ring gauge 50 (19.84 mm), length 178 mm (7 inches)

Perfecto unico: ring gauge 38 (15,08 mm), length 115 mm (4½ inches)

Corona gorda: ring gauge 46 (18.26 mm), length 143 mm (5⅝ inches)

Demi-tasse: ring gauge 28 (11,11 mm), length 132 mm (5¼ inches)

Epicure : ring gauge 50 (19.84 mm), length 132 mm (5¼ inches)

No IV: ring gauge 46 (18.26 mm), length 143 mm (5⅝ inches)

JOHN AYLESBURY

*I*n Germany demand for non-Cuban hand-made cigars is bigger than that for Havanas. The John Aylesbury Society was set up in 1974 by a group of German retailers with a commitment to selling high-quality tobacco products. As well as making cigars in Germany (from Brazilian and Indonesian leaf), it also imports exclusive hand-made cigars from the Dominican Republic (Casa de Campo), fuller bodied Hondurans (Pedro de Alvarado and Santa Rosa de Copan) and Nicaraguans (Carlo Corado and Don Marco). Villaverde cigars are made in the Canary Islands. All have their own packaging and bands (the Dominican Embajador and Santo Domingo cigar bands actually say 'John Aylesbury'), and many of them are of excellent quality.

EMBAJADOR: RING GAUGE **50 (19,84 mm)**, LENGTH **127 mm (5 inches)**

JOYO DE NICARAGUA

*I*n the 1970s, prior to the development of the Dominican and Honduran industries, Nicaraguan cigars, particularly this brand, were considered by many to be the best non-Cubans certainly by those who liked full-bodied smokes. Then, because of civil war and economic problems (not helped by an American embargo), production was seriously affected, and quality fell off. There was a recovery in the mid-1990s, but Nicaraguan cigars were still not what they were. However, there has been a major resurgence in the Nicaraguan industry in the last few years, with quality back to what it was in the old days.

The Joyo de Nicaragua brand was launched in 1970 and is now made by Tobacos Puros de Nicaragua. It was re-launched in 2002 as Joyo de Nicaragua Antano 1970 to celebrate the success of the 1970 launch. The wrappers are oily Cuban seed hybrids. These are very full-bodied cigars of high quality, made in limited quantities, and are in great demand. Not surprisingly - *Cigar Insider* gave one a 91 rating. There are currently just a few sizes. The bands are more ornate than those of the old range.

CHURCHILL: RING GAUGE **48 (19.05 mm)**, LENGTH **175 mm (6⅞ inches)**

ELEGANTE: RING GAUGE **38 (15,08 mm)**, LENGTH **178 mm (6½ inches)**

Juan Clemente

This brand was founded in 1982 by French cigar lover Jean Clement. Made in the Dominican Republic, it has improved and developed over the years. In the past, construction has sometimes lead to poor draw. But that problem has been gradually, but not consistently, sorted out. There are now three ranges all with Connecticut Shade wrappers. The mild and fragrant Classic line (nine sizes), of which the Rothschild and Obelisco (a *figurado*) are the best, have yellow bands. The whopping Gargantua, 330mm/13 inches long, with a ring gauge of 50/19.8mm, added in the mid-1990s, has sensibly been dropped. The Club Selection line, with darker wrappers, shows the brand at its mellow best. The four sizes (the No. 2 is the most successful) are fuller bodied, and come with white bands. The most recent line is the Reserve series of four aged sizes: these are spicy and have red bands. The band on Juan Clementes is, most unusually, applied to the foot of the cigar, securing a piece of foil, which helps to protect these reasonably priced cigars.

Club Selection No. 2: ring gauge 46 (18.26 mm), length 115 mm (4½ inches)

La Invicta

This brand of well-made, mellow, medium-bodied cigars with a fairly delicate, spicy, slightly sweet flavour is made in Honduras for the renowned British importers Hunters & Frankau. It now comes in nine sizes - enough to cater for either long or short smokes - as opposed to six, with mostly different names, in the past. The wrappers are light to medium in colour and have a pleasant bouquet. There is a *maduro* version of the Petit Corona size. They are very reasonably priced and are only sold in cellophane bundles of twenty five. They are not the finest connoisseurs' cigars, but good for everyday smoking. La Invicta was once made in Jamaica.

Epicure: ring gague 50 (19,84 mm), length 115 mm (4½ inches)

Macanudo is easily the best-selling premium cigar brand in the United States, and one of the most popular in the world. There is even a Macanudo Club in New York. The name was first used for a size (particularly popular in Britain) of the Cuban Punch brand - and in fact Macanudo is essentially an offshoot of Punch. It was created by the Palicio company (then owners of Punch) during the Second World War for the British market. At the time, exchange controls meant that Cuban cigars could no longer be imported into Britain, so Palicio created the Macanudo brand in

MACANUDO

Jamaica (then a British colony) so that it could come within the Sterling area. At first, Macanudos had Cuban wrappers. Even today, the lid labels of the Havana Punch brand and Macanudo are very similar. The Spanish word *macanaudo*, usually used only by Argentinians, means 'fine and dandy', 'the best' or 'the ultimate'.

General Cigar bought the brand, and the Temple Hall factory where it was made, in 1968. After the blend was changed, with the help of Ramon Cifuentes, Macanudo was launched in America in 1971. In 1983, production of the brand also began in Santiago, in the Dominican Republic increasing hugely in the 1990s boom. General Cigar pulled out of Jamaica in 2000, and today all Macanudos are made in the Dominican Republic.

Macanudo's success as a brand has been helped by the introduction of a number of new lines over the years. Today there are four regular series - all of them known for their consistency and dependable high quality.

The original line is now called Macanudo Cafe. There are 22 sizes to choose from. They are elegant and well-made, and the smooth, mellow flavour appeals to many beginners as well as to connoisseurs who like a mild daytime smoke, though some find them low on aroma. Wrappers are of silky Connecticut Shade leaf, binders from the San Andres area of Mexico, and the filler blend is a mixture of Mexican and Dominican tobacco. The cigars mostly have names with British connotations (Hyde Park, Ascot, Prince Philip) with a couple of sizes (Hampton Court and Portofino) available in smart white tubes. The Diplomat, with its 60 ring gauge (23.6 mm), is a very thick, but short, *figurado*. A special feature of the Macanudos with shade wrappers is that the leaves are aged twice: once in the Dominican Republic, then back for a 'Winter Sweat', in the cool of Connecticut before being shipped back to the factory. Some Macanudo sizes are unavailable internationally.

Macanudos as a whole are relatively expensive. Those with red bands and sold as Macanudo Vintage are particularly costly, liked by connoisseurs for their rich, nutty flavour. Vintage cigars are distinguished by their superb wrappers, and are made in limited numbers. They were first introduced in 1989, using aged tobacco from the 1979 harvest (the vintage refers to a year in which particularly good wrappers were grown, not to the year of production). The other leaves in these cigars are also specially aged. Other vintage years, so far, are 1984, 1988, 1993 and 1997. The year of the vintage is shown on a second band. The last few cigars from the 1979 vintage went on sale for £220 each at the Macanudo Fumoir in Claridge's Hotel in London at the end of 2003: very much cigars for the collector, priced according to their age.

DUKE OF DEVON: RING GAUGE 42 (16.67 mm), LENGTH 139 mm (5 ½ inches)

DUKE OF WINDSOR: RING GAUGE 50 (19.84 mm), LENGTH 152 mm (6 inches)

PETIT CORONA: RING GAUGE 38 (15.08 mm), LENGTH 127 mm (5 inches)

CAFE CRYSTAL TUBOS: RING GAUGE 49 (19.45 mm), LENGTH 127 mm (5 inches)

IN 2003, A SPECIAL EDITION OF MACANUDO GOLD LABEL CIGARS CAME ON THE MARKET. THE FIVE SIZES, WITH AN ADDITIONAL GOLD BAND, ARE SWEET AND SMOOTH, MADE WITH SPECIALLY SELECTED CONNECTICUT SHADE WRAPPERS, MEXICAN BINDERS AND DOMINICAN CUBAN SEED AND MEXICAN FILLERS.

THE MACANUDO ROBUST LINE WAS LAUNCHED IN 1998. WITH EIGHT SIZES, TWO IN TUBES. THE CIGARS ARE NOTICEABLY STRONGER (MEDIUM BODIED) AND SPICIER THAN OTHER MACANUDOS, BUT ARE STILL VERY SMOOTH. THEY CARRY A DISTINCTIVE 'R' LOGO AND COME IN A STYLISH DARK GREEN BOX. A PET PROJECT OF GENERAL CIGAR'S EDGAR CULLMAN, THESE SUPERIOR CIGARS ARE MADE WITH DOMINICAN PILOTO CUBANO FILLER, HAVANA SEED BINDERS (GROWN IN CONNECTICUT), AND DARK AGED CONNECTICUT SHADE WRAPPERS. (SEE SECOND ON THE LEFT).

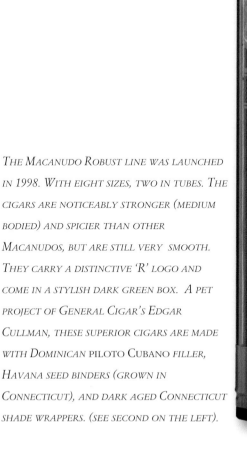

VINTAGE NO. VIII: RING GAUGE 50 (19.84 mm), LENGTH 139 mm (5 ½ inches)

ROBUST HYDE PARK: RING GAUGE 49 (19.45 mm), LENGTH 139 mm (5 ½ inches)

ROBUST BARON ROTHSCHILD: RING GAUGE 42 (16.67 mm), LENGTH 166 mm (6 ½ inches)

VINTAGE NO. IV: RING GAUGE 47 (18.65 mm), LENGTH 115 mm (4 ½ inches)

MADURO PRINCE PHILIP: RING GAUGE 49 (19.45 mm), LENGTH 192 mm (7 ½ inches)

MADURO HAMPTON COURT: RING GAUGE 42 (16.67 mm), LENGTH 139 mm (5 ½ inches)

CAFE PRINCE OF WALES: RING GAUGE 52 (20.64 mm), LENGTH 203 mm (8 inches)

CAFE DUKE OF WELLINGTON: RING GAUGE 47 (18.65 mm), LENGTH 216 mm (8 ½ inches)

THE MADURO LINE, LAUNCHED IN 1999 DIFFERS FROM PREVIOUS MADURO MACANUDOS MADE IN THE 1970s WITH MEXICAN BINDERS. THE CURRENT MADUROS ARE RICHER, AND USE CONNECTICUT BROADLEAF WRAPPERS WITH AN ATTRACTIVE SHEEN. BINDERS ARE CONNECTICUT SHADE, AND THE FILLERS LEAVES ARE DOMINICAN AND MEXICAN (SAN ANDRES). THESE PEPPERY, SLIGHTLY SWEET CIGARS COME IN SEVEN SIZES AND SPORT THE LETTER M ON THEIR BANDS. (SEE FIRST CIGAR ON LEFT).

PADRON

*P*adrons, although produced in very limited numbers, are possibly the finest cigars made in Nicaragua. They have achieved high ratings in tastings, and a devoted following among connoisseurs. Despite this they are reasonably priced.

Founded by Cuban exile, Jose O. Padron in Miami, the company has made cigars since 1964. Padron started production in Nicaragua in 1970, and also opened a factory in Danli, Honduras in 1977. After President Reagan's embargo on Nicaragua in 1985, all production moved to Honduras, but the Padrons started making cigars in Nicaragua again in 1990. They now have a new factory in Esteli. They grow their own Cuban seed Nicaraguan tobacco, and ensure the finest quality control and consistency.

The basic line, the Padron, available in 13 sizes, comes in both natural and *maduro* wrappers. The tobacco for these medium to full-bodied cigars is aged for two and a half years. The more complex Padron 1964 Anniversary series, launched in 1994, has nine sizes (with both natural and *maduro* wrappers). The leaf is aged at least four years. They are smooth, rich and medium-bodied.

The fuller-bodied Padron Millennium celebrated the year 2000. Using tobacco aged for five years, the cigar is 152mm/6 inches long with a 52 ring gauge (20.5mm), and only 100,000 were made. The equally full-bodied Serie 1926, also made with leaf aged for five years, was produced to celebrate the 75th birthday of Jose Padron.

ANNIVERSARIO DIPLOMATICO : RING GAUGE 50 (19.84 mm), LENGTH 178 mm (7 inches)

ANNIVERSARIO IMPERIAL: RING GAUGE 54 (16.67 mm), LENGTH 152 mm (6 inches)

ANNIVERSARIO TORPEDO: RING GAUGE 52 (20.64 mm), LENGTH 152 mm (6 inches)

ANNIVERSARIO PRINCIPE NATURAL: RING GAUGE 46 (18.26 mm), LENGTH 115 mm (4½ inches)

PAUL GARMIRIAN

$\mathcal{P}$aul Garmirian's P.G. cigars are not that easy to find, and nor are they cheap, but they are some of the best non-Havanas around. Garmirian has a Ph.D in international politics and used to be a real-estate agent until the success of his brand, launched in 1991, led him to go into the cigar business full-time. He is recognized as a leading cigar expert, partly because of his book The Gourmet Guide to Cigars (1990). He teamed up with one of the world's greatest cigar producers, Hendrik Kelner (who also supervised the Davidoff, Avo and Griffin's brands), to create his own Dominican marque.

There were originally only six sizes, but now the basic line, the Gourmet series has 20. They have oily, reddish-brown Connecticut Shade wrappers and Dominican fillers and binders. They are very well constructed and burn well with a subtle bouquet, and a spicy, mellow (though medium to full-bodied) flavour. The Maduro series (six sizes) has Dominican and Brazilian fillers, Indonesian binders and Connecticut Broadleaf wrappers.

The fuller-bodied Gourmet Series II was launched in 1999, with just two sizes, Torpedo and Robusto. The Connoisseur and Belicoso Fino were added in late 2001. The Reserva Exclusiva series (made from ten year old tobacco) was also launched that year in the Corona and Belicoso sizes, joined by three others in 2002. They are full and rich, made with Dominican and Ecuadorian fillers, Dominican binders and Ecuadorian wrappers.

LONSDALE: RING GAUGE **42** (16,67 mm), LENGTH **165 mm** (6 ½ inches)

BELICOSO: RING GAUGE **52** (20,64 mm), LENGTH **165 mm** (6 ½ inches)

CHURCHILL: RING GAUGE **48** (19,05 mm), LENGTH **178 mm** (7 inches)

DOUBLE CORONA: RING GAUGE **50** (19,84 mm), LENGTH **194 mm** (7 ⅝ inchehs)

PETRUS

$\mathcal{L}$aunched in 1990, this high quality brand is popular in Europe; founded by Switz-American Philip Gregory Wynne. The blend, and range, has changed since it first appeared. The basic line (once made in Honduras) is now made in Nicaragua, with Nicaraguan leaf, including Connecticut seed sun-grown wrappers. The cigars (five sizes) are mild to medium bodied, with a spicy, coffee flavour. The Royal Maduro series (three sizes) has red bands, and is made in the Dominican Republic. The cigars (with *piloto Cubano* binders and fillers) are richer and more powerful. The most sophisticated and expensive is the Petrus Fortus line: strong, satisfying, but subtle, with black and red bands. Also Dominican-made, the wrappers are dark Ecuadorian Broadleaf, the binders *piloto Cubano*, and the filler a blend of *piloto Cubano* (Cuban seed) and Brazilian *mata fina*.

ROTHSCHILD: RINGMASS **50 (19,84 mm)**, LÄNGE **121 mm (5 inches)**

PLEIADES

$\mathcal{O}$riginally produced for SEITA, the French state tobacco monopoly (now part of Altadis), in 1984, these are generally mild, smooth but flavourful cigars, with an attractive aroma. They look good and are well-made in the Dominican Republic. Filler leaves (*olor Domicano* and *piloto Cubano*) come from the Cibao valley, and they have Connecticut Shade wrappers. Once they are manufactured (at Santiago de Los Caballeros), the cigars are transported to Strasbourg, and aged for six months, after which they are placed in boxes with a built-in humidifying system, before being distributed in Europe. Those exported to the United States are now sent directly there. They are named after planets and constellations.

Changes were made to the range and blend in late 2000. There is an extensive range of over a dozen sizes. The best sizes are the Orion, Perseus, Aldebaran, and the peppery Andares. The Peleiades Reserve Privee 1992 is a limited edition of impressive aged cigars.

URANUS : RING GAUGE **34 (13,49 mm)**, LENGTH **175 mm (6 ⅞inches)**

ALDEBARAN: RING GAUGE **50 (19.84 mm)**, LENGTH **216 mm (8 ½inches)**

SANTA DAMIANA

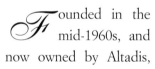

*O*nce a well-known Havana brand, Santa Damiana cigars have been made at La Romana, in the Dominican Republic, since 1993. The brand is now owned by Altadis. Santa Damianas destined for the United States have different names and sizes from those available in Europe, and the range is smaller. Those sold in America have numbers (No. 100 and so on), while those on sale in Europe have traditional names (such as Churchill, Corona and Robusto). Eight sizes (including two in yellow tubes) are available in Europe, but only five (pretty fat) sizes in the United States. All the cigars are well-made, and have elegant blue and gold bands. They have a delicate, slightly spicy flavour, and a pleasing aroma. The brand as a whole ranges from mild to medium, and the cigars are made with Dominican filler, Dominican binders, and Connecticut Shade wrappers. These are well-made cigars with what used to be thought of as a typical Dominican flavour, and are very good of their type.

SELECCION 300: RING GAUGE **42** (16,67 mm), LENGTH **127 mm (5 inches)**

TE AMO

*F*ounded in the mid-1960s, and now owned by Altadis, this is perhaps the best known Mexican brand - certainly in the United States - originally much-smoked by rag trade workers in New York's Garment District. The cigars once had a reputation for a roughish flavour, but now their coarse wrappers have gone, the construction is good, and Te-Amos are considered stylish. They come in a range of sizes in the basic range (17 altogether), and in a choice of light brown or *maduro* wrappers. All the tobaccos used are Mexican, from the San Andres Valley. The fuller Aniversario series (six sizes with some *maduro* versions and *figurados*) is particularly good (the *maduro* Toro was rated 91 by Cigar Aficionado). They have Habana 2000 wrappers, Mexican binders, and a filler blend of Nicaraguan, Dominican and Mexican Cuban seed tobacco. The Cabinet Selection (five large girth sizes) are wrapped with Mexican Sumatra tobacco (the *maduros* wrappers and binders are Mexican grown Habana 2000) and the fillers a blend of Mexican, Brazilian and Dominican leaves, so they're punchy cigars. The simple red bands have gone, and now feature a matador and bull, unavailable as we went to press.

No. 4: RING GAUGE **42** (16,67 mm), LENGTH **127 mm (5 inches)**

This high-quality brand was created by the great Zino Davidoff for the American market when Davidoff cigars were still being produced in Cuba, and thus unavailable in the United States. Zinos have been sold internationally for many years, however, and can be found at the many Davidoff shops around the world, as well as other retailers. The original line, made in Honduras, and dressed with gold bands, was medium bodied. The mild to medium, but aromatic and nutty Mouton Cadet series, with its distinctive dark red bands, was launched in the 1983 and promoted at the time by Baroness Phillipine de Rothschild, whose family produce the eponymous claret. There were only three cigars originally, but the range has been extended to ten sizes, mainly numbered, and many of them available in tubes. But some sizes aren't available everywhere. The latest addition is the Torpedo (130mm/5 ⅛ inches x 50/19.8mm). The No. 6 is a *robusto*. The series is made in Honduras with Ecuadorian Connecticut wrappers, and Honduran binders and fillers. They're by no means cheap, but prices are fairly reasonable given the quality. The Connoisseur series was specially produced to celebrate the opening of the Davidoff shop in Madison Avenue in New York in 1987, and continued for several years. It consisted of four fuller bodied cigars with large ring gauges. There are also several machine-made Zinos using Brazilian and Indonesian tobacco.

The latest development in the brand is the introduction of the two Platinum series. The first, Platinum Crown, came on to the American market at the end of 2002 - at staggeringly high prices. But, despite their cost, the cigars were an almost immediate success, though not widely available. The Platinum Scepter series, launched in the middle of 2003, is notably less expensive. Both series are gradually becoming available in Europe - in Germany, Switzerland, Russia and Britain, for instance. The introduction of Platinum cigars was very much a matter of marketing. The concept started with brand consultants Peter Arnell and Steve Stout, and was developed along with Davidoff's CEO Dr. Reto Cina, a man with a background in cosmetics, not cigars. The idea was to position the cigars (a joint venture between Davidoff, Arnell and Stout) not only as luxury status symbols at the very top of the market, but also to attract younger, hipper people, who might not have smoked cigars before. The Scepter series, aimed further down the market, benefits from the cachet of the name, and the publicity gained by the Crown. The names of the cigars (Chubby, Low Rider and Shorty, for instance, for Scepters) are an obvious attempt to sound hip.

The two series are differently, though fancily, packaged: the Scepters in cans, the Crowns in small boxes with metal matchbooks. The Crowns now come in four sizes (there were originally three), all of which have huge ring gauges (the largest is the latest, the Barrel, 62/24.3mm), whilst the Scepters are made in five sizes, and are somewhat smaller. Both are produced in the Dominican Republic, under the supervision of master cigar maker, Hendrik Kelner. The lines are likely to be developed further, and the Zino brand, as a whole, might change.

ZINO

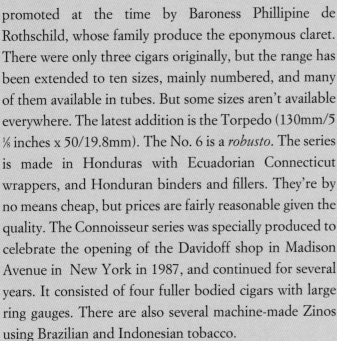

MOUTON CADET NO. 1: RING GAUGE 44 (17,46 mm), LENGTH 166 mm (6½ inches)

MOUTON CADET NO. 5: RING GAUGE 42 (16,67 mm), LENGTH 127 mm (5 inches)

MOUTON CADET NO. 6: RING GAUGE 50 (19,84 mm), LENGTH 127 mm (5 inches)

MOUTON CADET TORPEDO: RING GAUGE 54 (21,44 mm), LENGTH 132 mm (5¼ inches)

THE FILLER LEAVES FOR PLATINUM
CIGARS ARE AGED FOR AT LEAST FOUR
YEARS, AND CONSIST OF THREE TYPES OF
DOMINICAN TOBACCO, AND A PERUVIAN
LEAF NOT USED BEFORE BY DAVIDOFF.
THE BINDERS ARE CONNECTICUT SHADE,
AND WRAPPERS ARE CONNECTICUT SEED
ECUADORIAN, FERMENTED FOR A YEAR.
THE FLAVOUR IS DISTINCTLY FULL,
INTENSE, COMPLEX AND SMOOTH. THE
BAND OF THE ZINO PLATINUM RANGE IS
SHOWN ON PAGE 160

CIGAR LISTS

Opoosite DIFFERENT TIME OF DAY, DIFFERENT

CIGAR, SEE PAGE 164.

A MISCELLANY OF cigar information, from the favourite smokes of leading figures in the cigar world to the author's practical tips on choosing and smoking cigars.

BRUCE LEWIS'S CHOICE OF CIGARS FOR DIFFERENT TIMES OF THE DAY

*B*RUCE LEWIS is International Development Manager of General Cigar International. He has spent his entire working life immersed in tobacco, with a particular passion for hand-crafted cigars. As the Director of International Business Development for General Cigar, he travels the world visiting tobacco farms, factories, distributors and retailers sampling cigars of all shapes, style and taste. He has run hundreds of master classes on cigars and is regularly invited to speak on the subject at a variety of functions. Not surprisingly, Bruce greatly enjoys his job.

• My first cigar in the morning after arriving at the office is either a Macanudo Hyde Park Cafe or Macanudo Vintage 1997 No.II. Both of these cigars are quite mild and have a very pleasant flavour. The Cafe is creamy with a good 'cedar wood' finish while the Vintage is very elegant and refined. Perfect with a good cup of English breakfast tea.

• After lunch I enjoy lighting up a Macanudo Diplomat Maduro with a cup of Espresso. This cigar is medium-bodied and has excellent depth and complexity of flavour. The flavour has a core of sweet spice and the long, lingering finish has strong notes of earth and leather. The sweetness of this cigar compliments the bitterness of the strong coffee.

• Before dinner I prefer a cigar, which will go well with a pre-dinner drink, especially a glass of champagne or a Martini. I particularly enjoy the Hoyo de Monterrey Excalibur Perfect Unico which is full of flavour, yet retains excellent balance and smoothness. Its taste has a certain nuttiness and the wooded finish has a lovely creamy texture. It won't exhaust the palate before eating.

• After dinner I really enjoy a strong cigar, but, just as important, it must have rich, complex flavours, especially as I like cognac or aged rum with my final cigar of the day. So my usual choice is the El Credito Torpedo No. 2 Natural. This is a medium- to full-bodied cigar, which has a beautiful solid core of spice and pepper. The finish is long, spicy and leathery. If I am in the mood for an even richer, bolder, more complex and robust cigar, then the obvious choice is the new El Credito Serie R No. 6.

ABOVE: BRUCE LEWIS.
OPPOSITE: MARLENE DIETRICH

Simon Chases's favourite Havanas

Outside Cuba very few people know more about Havana cigars than Simon Chase, Marketing Director of British cigar importer Hunters & Frankau. His knowledge, enthusiasm and experience has guided several authors of internationally published cigar books, and he influenced the development of Cigar Aficianado magazine.

He says: "After nearly 30 years in the Havana trade, it's no easier to pick just ten cigars. All these have given me particular pleasure at one time or another, and have proved reliable over time."

MY TOP TEN

Ramon Allones Specially Selected
When asked which cigar I'd choose before facing the firing squad, this remains my selection. It's a traditional robusto with rich, earthy flavours for those exceptional moments, not every day.

Partagas Lusitania
Maybe this is a better choice before the firing squad, as it's longer. Another rich cigar. Its length means that you experience a remarkable range of flavours as you smoke it. Go for a cigar from a Cabinet Selection bundle of 50.

Montecristo No. 2
This is the definitive Piramide or Torpedo, often challenged by other brands but seldom beaten.

Punch Petit Corona del Punch
This is my preferred choice for a Petit Corona or Mareva because, most of all, it has proved consistent despite facing some difficult times.

Cuaba Divinos
A relatively new addition to my list, after all it was only introduced in 1996. A spicy, short smoke to wake up the palate with your morning coffee.

Cohiba Siglo III
This proved my favourite on the night we launched the Siglo range in London back in 1993, and it still is. Be warned, however, few people agree with me.

Cohiba Reserva Piramide
This is a Piramide to challenge the Monte No. 2. Rare, and not cheap, but worth the hunt and the investment. All the tobaccos were aged for three years before they were made into cigars at the end of 2002.

Romeo y Julieta Cedros No. 1
Still a favourite, this is Romeo's only Lonsdale. Its cedar wrap gives it a particular delicacy.

Partagas Short
Another spicy, short smoke with a good ring gauge. I used to prefer them from Cabinet Selection 50 bundles, but the label box version is proving just as good these days.

Trinidad Coloniales
This is a real newcomer; it arrived on the scene as recently as 2003. Raul Valladares, who created the blend, went  for fragrance and aroma, and got both. A great smoke for the summer months.

NOTABLE WOMEN CIGAR SMOKERS

Drew Barrymore	Madonna
Marlene Dietrich	Demi Moore
Linda Evangelista	George Sand
Whoopi Goldberg	Claudia Schiffer
Lauren Hutton	Virginia Woolf

Top ten cigars sold at auction at Christie's

Christie's in London have held specialist cigar auctions twice a year since May 1999. Before that date, cigars were sold as part of wine sales. There are roughly 300 to 400 boxes in each sale. According to Christie's cigar auctioneer (and wine expert) Brian Ebbesen, these are the top saleroom prices achieved for Havana cigars in the last few years.

- Partagas Lusitanias '109' (pointed end) Pre-embargo. 3 cigars in a cardboard box. Sold for £3,300 per 3 cigars, a world record.

- Davidoff 80th Aniversario (1986). Cabinet of 10 cigars. Sold for £8,500 per 10 cigars.

- Davidoff 80th Aniversario (1986). Cabinet of 20 cigars. Sold for £13,000 per 20 cigars.

- Dunhill Cabinetta (mid 1980s). Sold for £6,000 per 25 cigars.

- Partagas Lusitanias 150th Aniversario (limited run of 11 boxes of 25 cigars only, from 1995) Sold for £3,600 per 25 cigars.

- Ramon Allones Gigantes '109' (pointed end) from 1975. Sold for £3,600 per 25 cigars.

- Partagas Churchills. 1 cabinet of 100 from 1973. Sold for £12,000 per 100 cigars and again for £10,000 per 100 cigars.

- Montecristo Seleccion Suprema No 1. Cabinet of 100 cigars. Sold for £7,000 per 100 cigars.

- Davidoff Chateau Lafite. Cabinet of 50. Sold for £1,600 per 50 cigars.

- Davidoff Chateau Haut-Brion. Cabinet of 50 sold for £1,500 per 50 cigars.

Possibly the ten most expensive cigars on sale at Davidoff in London

This list of course went out of date almost soon as it was written, but it is nonetheless a useful indication of the priciest cigars sold internationally; prices per cigar were correct as this book went to press.

- Cuaba Diademas (Limited Edition) - £39.80
- Cohiba Double Corona (Limited Edition) - £33.48
- Montecristo "A" - £31.04
- Hoyo de Monterrey Particulares (Limited Edition) - £29
- Davidoff Aniversario No. 1 Tubos
- (Dominican) - £29
- Cohiba Esplendido - £25.92
- Davidoff Double "R" (Dominican) - £25.76
- Cohiba Piramides (Limited Edition) - £23.88
- Cuaba Salomon (Limited Edition) - £22.30
- Montecristo Double Coronas (Limited Edition) - £21.20

These are all cigars with large ring gauges (47-55). By rearranging the list in terms of size (length and ring gauge), it emerges which cigars are the most expensive per puff:

Cohiba Double Corona
Cohiba Esplendido
Cuaba Diademas
Cohiba Piramides
Montecristo "A"
Davidoff Aniversario No. 1 Tubos
Davidoff Double "R"
Hoyo de Monterrey Particulares
Montecristo Double Corona
Cuaba Salomon

Other pricey cigars

In late 1996, entrepreneur Peter de Savary bought 163 Havanas made, in 1857 and 1858, for the Duke of Buccleuch, for £17,600 at Christie's -that is, £108 each.

In May 1997, a box of 25 Trinidads (not then available commercially) went for £6,924 in an auction in Geneva - £277 a cigar.

Later in 1997, one of the 501 limited edition 1492 humidors made in 1992, to commemorate Columbus's voyage 500 years earlier, made £15,000 - or £300 each for the *corona gorda* cigars inside. When they first appeared, the boxes sold for only £850.

In November 1997, a box of 25 Trinidads (before the brand was available commercially) was sold in Geneva for £9,890 - or £395 each.

In May 1999, two boxes of five pre-Revolutionary Hoyo de Monterrey 9 1/4 inch *figurados*, once owned by Hector Ayala, former Cuban ambassador to France, sold for £3,100 each. That is, £620 per cigar

In the late 1990s, Sandy Perceval offered 600 cigars (500 of them in good condition) dating from 1864. The property of an ancestor, they had been kept in humid cellar in the family's home, Temple House in Sligo, Ireland. At the time, the cigars were much hyped, but experts eventually decided that they were from the Philippines, rather than Cuba. That didn't stop an American enthusiast offering $1 million for them.

The last few Macanudo cigars from the 1979 vintage were on sale at the Fumoir at Claridge's hotel in London in late 2003 for £220 each.

Rare post-revolution cuban brands and cigars

These are brands, or sizes, which have been discontinued, or cigars of current brands produced for special occasions in special sizes.

- Belinda (hand made, long filler - discontinued in 1960s)
- Bolivar Gold Medal (half wrapped in gold coloured foil - discontinued 1992)
- Cohiba 30th Aniversario (1996). And pre-1992 •
- Cohibas
- Cohiba Piramide
- Cuaba Distinguidos
- Davidoff Chateau Mouton Rothschild
- Davidoff Dom Perignon
- Dunhill Atado
- Dunhill Estupendo
- Dunhill Malecon
- Dunhill Mojito
- Dunhill Varadero
- Hoyo de Monterrey Obsequios (discontinued in 1970s)
- Hoyo de Monterrey Opera (discontinued in 1980s)
- Hoyo de Monterrey Odeon (discontinued in 1980s)
- H. Upmann Crystales (sold in glass jars - discontinued early 1990s)
- Jose L. Piedra (long filler - pre 1990s)
- La Escepcion
- Montecristo Robusto
- Partagas Fabulosos (discontinued in the early 1970s)
- Partagas Salomones No II
- Por Larranaga Magnum
- Romeo y Julieta Fabulosos (discontinued late 1980s)
- Siboney (only one size)

THE TEN BEST-SELLING CIGARS AT THE DAVIDOFF SHOP IN LONDON

Montecristo No. 4
Montecristo No. 3
Montecristo No. 2
Cohiba Robusto
Partagas Series D. No. 4
Hoyo de Monterrey Epicure no. 2
Cohiba Siglo II
Davidoff Special "R"
Davidoff No. 2
H. Upmann Corona Junior

BELOW: THE OLD GENEVA DAVIDOFF SHOP.

EDWARD SAHAKIAN'S TEN FAVOURITE CIGARS

Edward Sahakian, owner of the Davidoff shop in London, is one of the world's best-known and respected cigar retailers. He is also famous for his enthusiasm for cigars and willingness to share his considerable knowledge. "I like mild cigars through choice, so my selection is of cigars on the milder side," he says.

Davidoff No. 3 (Dominican)
Davidoff No. 2 (Dominican)
Cohiba Panetela (Cuban)
Trinidad Reyes (Cuban)
Hoyo de Monterry Double Corona (Cuban)
Cohiba Corona Especial (Cuban)
Avo Allegro (Dominican)
Paul Garmirian Especial (Dominican)
H. Upmann Corona Junior (Cuban)
Trinidad Robusto Extra (Cuban)

"The true smoker abstains from imitating Vesuvius." - **Auguste Barthelemy**

"When a wife can purchase her husband the right cigars, their relationship is blessed." - **Colette**

"A well-chosen cigar is like armour and is useful against the torments of life. A little blue smoke mysteriously removes anxiety." - **Zino Davidoff**

"If the birth of a genius resembles that of an idiot, the end of a Havana Corona resembles that of a fie cent cigar." - **Sacha Guitry**

"If you are obsessed by sad thoughts, a cigar will take your mind off them..." - **Duc De La Rochefoucauld**

"The best cigar ... is wrapped in a leaf that does not dissolve in the mouth, and which keeps its aroma to the end." - **Somerset Maugham**

"Any cigar smoker is a friend, because I know what he feels." - **Alfred de Musset**

"Cigars calm pain and people loneliness with a thousand gracious images." - **George Sand**

"I vow and believe that the cigar has been one of the greatest creature-comforts of my life - a kind companion, a gentle stimulant, an amiable anodyne, a cementer of friendship." - **William Makepeace Thackeray**

"The cigar, like the pipe, ought to match your physique." - **Kees Van Dongen**

"The most futile and disastrous day seems well spent when it is reviewed through the blue, fragrant smoke of a Havana" - **Evelyn Waugh**

"I would rather die with a cigar in my mouth than boots on my feet" - **Darryl F. Zanuck**

In the U.S.A., of course, Cuban cigars are not on sale.

Macanudo (Dominican Republic)

Punch (Honduras)

Partagas (Dominican Republic)

La Gloria Cubana (Dominikanische Republik)

Hoyo de Monterrey/Excalibur (Honduras)

Hoyo de Monterrey (Dominican Republic)

Fuente (Dominican Republic)

Montecristo (Dominican Republic)

Romeo y Julieta (Dominican Republic)

Davidoff (Dominican Republic)

Padron (Nicaragua)

Anwer Bati's 12 tips for choosing cigars

1 It is best to compare cigars in similar conditions.

2 The wrapper should have a slight sheen and should be smooth and undamaged, without any noticeable veins. It shouldn't be too brittle or dry but should be firm to the touch, although not too stiff. The cigar should give a little when gently pressed between finger and thumb, but spring back into shape. An over-soft cigar will be poorly filled and burn too fast; a cigar which is too firm will draw badly.

3 If you're buying a box of cigars, check the contents. The bands should all be in the same position and the spirals on the wrapper leaves should all face the same direction. They should be the same basic colour, with the lightest shades on the right and the darkest on the left. Small white spots and green patches are normal.

4 Before you smoke take into account the brand, country of origin, size, appearance and bouquet. Whilst you smoke observe the flavour, quality of burning and the draw, which should be easy and the smoke should be not too hot or acrid. This is dependent on the quality of the cigar's construction.

5 Cigars with larger ring gauges (*corona* and above) and specialist sizes such as figurados are made by the most experienced rollers and so are better made than the rest of the range, offering a slower, smoother smoke. As a result they are relatively more expensive.

6 It is the filler blend, rather than the wrapper, that determines flavour. Manufacturers often 'label' the flavour of their cigars by their choice of wrapper colour - dark wrappers often indicate fuller-bodied cigars, and lighter onese (particularly Connecticut Shade), milder cigars. This is not always true, however.

7 Many serious cigar smokers prefer to smoke a mild cigar in the morning, reserving fuller-bodied cigars for later in the day. The *robusto* size has become popular as a short, punchy smoke after a heavy lunch.

8 Smoking a strong cigar before eating will only diminish your appetite and appreciation of your food and wine.

9 Always move from mild cigars to strong - the other way makes no sense.

10 There is no such thing as the 'best' size to smoke. The Cubans have an old saying, 'as you approach 30, you have a 30 ring gauge; as you approach 50, you have a 50 ring gauge.'

11 There is no such thing as the 'best cigar' - although there is such a thing as the most expensive. Brands such as Cohiba are often sold at high prices to reflect their status rather than quality alone. The best cigar is the one you like most.

12 Beware of apparent bargains - you may be getting fakes, machine-made sizes of Cuban brands (often in cellophane); or Dominican or Honduran versions of Havana brands.

Anwer Bati's list of what to drink with cigars

Strong cigars: Cognac; Armagnac; Islay Whisky - such as Lagavulin or Ardbeg; Rum

Medium-bodied cigars: Port; Madeira; Medium-bodied sherry

Mild cigars: Light sherry; Highland malt whisky; Heavy red wine

ANWER BATI'S 15 TIPS FOR SMOKING CIGARS

1 Cut cigars, carefully, with something sharp.

2 Make the cut quick, clean and level, and leave the bottom of the cap intact to avoid damaging the wrapper. Cut *figurados* (pointed at both ends) in the same way.

3 Piercing the cap will compress the tobacco and make the cigar overheat.

4 Don't rush. Lighting a cigar is a skill. hold the foot of the cigar at aright angle to the flame, rotating it until evenly charred. next place the cigar between your lips and - keeping the flame just out of contact - draw on it, whilst rotating, until it is alight. Then blow on the rotating end gently to ensure it is evenly lit. Now you can smoke.

5 There is no need to char the foot end of a figurado - simply apply the flame and puff gently.

6 If you puff too often the cigar will overheat - smoke slowly.

7 Well matured cigars burn smoother than younger ones.

8 The very best cigars leave a much thinner carbon rim at the lit end than those of lower quality.

9 Choose a size suitable fo rthe amount of time you have - a medium-sized cigar (e.g. corona) should last half an hour.

10 Don't warm the length of the cigar before lighting it.

11 Don't stick your cigar in port or brandy - you will ruin it.

12 Don't 'listen to the band,' - rolling a cigar by your ear.

13 Don't remove the band until you have smoked the cigar for a few minutes as this could damage the wrapper.

14 An extinguished cigar is still OK to smoke a few hours later, particularly if it has a large ring gauge.

15 Before tapping the ash off your cigar, let roughly an inch-long cylinder of ash form, letting it fall into the ashtray.

Some top cigar shops

- ALFRED DUNHILL (Geneva , London, New York, Sydney and many other cities)
- ANDRINGA, Amsterdam
- DAS TABAKHAUS, Berlin
- DAVIDOFF (Amsterdam, Berlin, Geneva, Hong Kong, London, Montreal, New York)
- GEORGETOWN TOBACCO, Washington D.C.
- GERARD PERE ET FILS, Geneva
- GIMENO, Barcelona
- HAJENIUS, Amsterdam
- JAMES J. FOX & ROBERT LEWIS, London
- LA CASA DEL HABANO (Berlin, Cologne, Dusseldorf, and several other cities around the world)
- LA CIVETTE, Paris
- LINZBACH, Dusseldorf
- MAX ZECHBAUER, Munich
- NAT SHERMAN, New York
- SINCATO, Rome
- WOLSDORFF (Bonn, Dusseldof, Hamburg)
- CIGARNEWS.COM, a useful source of information for Casa Blanca and other U.S cigars

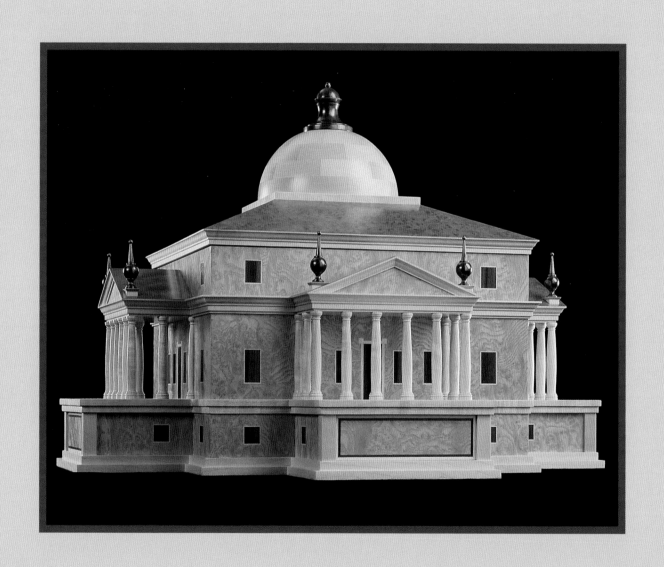

CIGAR ART & ACCESSORIES

THIS SECTION IS ABOUT beautiful cigar box decorations; the world's finest (priciest) cigar cutters; and humidors (see left, and pages 178, 179, 182-183 and 186-187 which can claim to be works of art.

THE COLOURFUL images (or "vistas") on box lids, cigar bands, and even the often gaudy border decorations on boxes (habilitaciones), inspire passion in some collectors, particularly if they can find original artwork. Ramon Allones was the first to use illustrations to adorn cigar boxes in the 1840s. Soon they took on an importance beyond mere embellishment - as a way of differentiating brands - as the cigar industry grew. They were originally printed using stone lithography, often in Germany, where the technique originated, before modern methods took over. Recently, the trend has been to use simpler designs - for brands such as Cohiba., Trinidad, Davidoff and Vegueros. However San Christobal, Vegas Robaina and others, maintain the traditional style. Special packaging has also been used, particularly for anniversary editions. A number of manufacturers have tried out new forms of packaging - the tin drums of the Zino Platinum Scepter series, for instance. A perennial favourite is the subtly-coloured vista on El Rey del Mundo boxes (see right).

Cigar bands were invented (probably in the 1860s) by Gustavo Bock, and their use quickly became widespread. It's possible that Bock decided to identify his Havanas with bands because, at the time, many German manufacturers were producing cigars, which they passed off as Cuban. Romeo y Julieta was the first Havana brand to introduce personalised bands, a notion which appealed to wealthy smokers. Many leading companies also had customised bands for their cigar supplies. Other bands were produced to celebrate special events or featured famous smokers. In Cuba the production of personalised bands generally stopped after the revolution, but Por Larranaga once produced bands with Che Guevara's portrait, and Cohibas - when they were gifts for foreign dignitaries - often carried the names of their recipients. A number of brands use more than one band. The Cuban Hoyo de Monterrey double *corona* has a fancier band than the rest of the range; and the Churchill size of Romeo y Julieta has a plain, narrow gold, rather than red, band. Brands such as Dunhill have different bands to show different countries of origin or lines.

The 1990s boom in cigar smoking led to the marketing of a staggering range of beautiful cigar accessories - some of them very expensive. Guillotine cutters come round, square or oblong in shape. They range from plastic, to those made of precious metals selling for hundreds of pounds. Cigar scissors are usually made of stainless steel, but their handles sometimes carry gold plate. Cigar lighters can cost from a couple of hundred pounds to a couple of thousand. You can also get silver match boxes, or match holders made in mahogany or leather. Ashtrays can sell for over £100. You can also find single cigar tubes in brass, gold or silver - sometimes lacquered. Small travelling humidors - made of wood, metal or leather - can normally fit into carry-on luggage. The best pocket cigar cases are made of leather, and are lined. Some cases come with small moisturising units.

Opposite Andy Warhol Limited Edition Series lighters by S.T. Dupont. Warhol gained fame in the 1960s using a screen-printing style of art, which mimicked commercial mass production techniques, to depict images of celebrities, such as Elvis Presley and Marilyn Monroe.

Below FLOR DE ALBA CAVE 200 HUMIDOR. THIS BEAUTIFUL HUMIDOR IS MADE BY THE FIRM ELLIE BLEU, WHO ARE FAMOUS FOR THEIR STRIKING DESIGNS. IT IS HAND-CRAFTED AND AVAILABLE IN NATURAL SYCAMORE, TINTED SYCAMORE (RED, BLUE, GREEN, GOLD YELLOW AND LIGHT YELLOW) AND MAHOGANY.

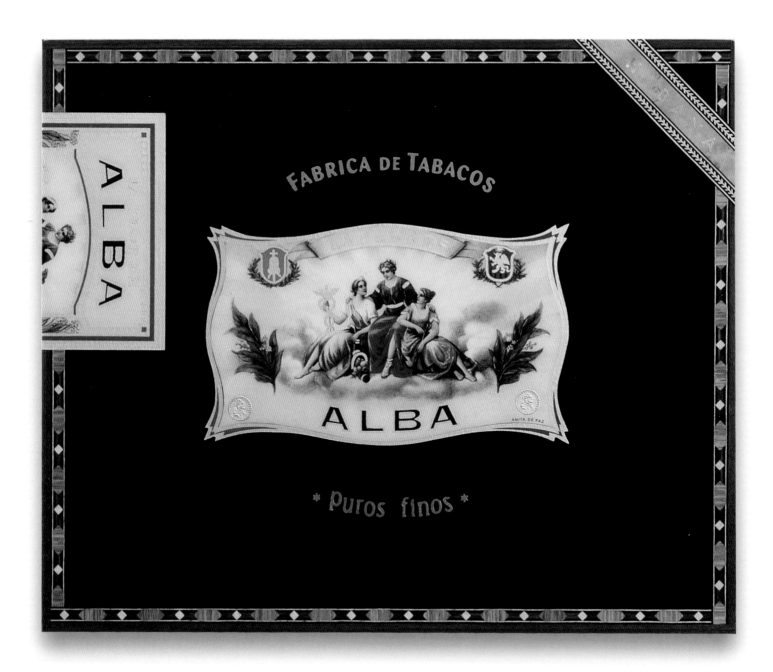

Left 'THE MEETING' HUMIDOR DESIGNED BY DAVID LINLEY FOR HIS 'ILLUSION SERIES'. HUMIDORS COST FROM UNDER A HUNDRED DOLLARS OR POUNDS (FOR PLASTIC AND ACRYLIC MODELS) TO MANY THOUSANDS - FOR WHAT ARE REALLY PIECES OR ORNAMENTAL FURNITURE, MADE OF WOODS SUCH AS MAHOGANY ANS WALNUT, LINED WITH CEDAR. LIMITED EDITION HUMIDORS MADE OF RARE WOODS, AND THOSE CUSTOM-MADE BY WELL-KNOWN DESIGNERS, SUCH AS DAVID LINELY COME AT LUXURIOUS PRICES.

Right 'THE OPENING', ANOTHER DAVID LINLEY HUMIDOR FROM HIS 'ILLUSION SERIES'. THIS REMARKABLE HUMIDOR APPEARS TO HAVE BEEN LEFT OPEN AND A DRAWER REMOVED. THE TROMPE-L'OEIL DESIGN WAS CREATED THROUGH THE SKILFUL USE OF MARGUETRY. IT TOOK OVER 300 HOURS TO ASSEMBLE AND REQIRED THE CUTTING OF OVER 1,700 INDIVIDUAL PIECES OF VENEER FROM A SELECTION OF 16 PRECIOUS WOODS, SUCH AS BLACK EBONY AND RED BURR AMBONY. IT CAN HOLD UP TO 300 CIGARS AND HAS A SECRET OPENING MECHANISM MADE POSSIBLE BY HAND-ENGINEERED FITTINGS AND LOCKS.

Above Dragon lighter. This magnificent, unusual lighter has a tail made of genuine blackbuck antelope horn, taken from original Victorian trophy heads dating back to the days of the Raj. Proud owners often use it as a centre piece in table decoration. Proud owners? You can only buy it from Harrods of London on special order - and it takes two months to come.

Left Carlos Torano Exodus 1959 box. The label in the lid reads: This cigar commemorates the Exodus of expert Cuban cigar families and their impact on the cigar industry after the nationalization of all tobacco farms and cigar factories by the Cuban government in 1959. The Torano were one of theose

Right Arturo Fuente Opus X box. These once-in-a-lifetime cigars were created by Carlos Fuente Jr. for his personal everday smoking. They are one of the most sought after and hardest to obtain cigars in the world due to limited production.

Left Sanit Luis Rey box art: Many vistas on cigar boxes feature portraits either of a brand's founder or famous personalities. Moments from Spanish history and royal emblems were also widely used, as were images of Cuban life, as seen here.

Left PARTAGAS HUMIDOR DESIGNED AND MADE BY BRITISH DESIGNER-CRAFSTMAN MARTIN LANE. MADE OF BUBINGA AND KEVASINGO, IT CONTAINS THREE PARTS, EACH OPENED BY A SECRET PUSH BUTTON. INSIDE ARE DRAWERS ON WHICH A VARIETY OF CIGAR BRAND LABLES HAVE BEEN LASER-ETCHED. OPPOSITE: BUBINGA CHEVRON HUMIDOR CABINET DESIGNED AND MADE BY MARTIN LANE AS A TRIBUTE TO ONE OF THE OLDEST HAVANA BRANDS. IT IS MADE OUT OF SYCAMORE, EBONY AND BELIZE CEDAR. ACROSS ALL THE DRAWER FRONTS IS A LASER-ETCHED PARTAGAS BRAND MARQUE.

Right OYSTER CHEST DESIGNED AND MADE BY MARTIN LANE. THIS HUMIDOR IS VENEERED IN WENGE AND THE TOP HAS 16 BOXWOOD OYSTERS, SEPERATED BY INLAID LINES OF EBONY AND BOXWOOD. THE INTERIOR IS LINED WITH HONDURAS CEDAR AND HAS A LIFT-OUT SLATTED TRAY AND MOVABLE PARTITION.

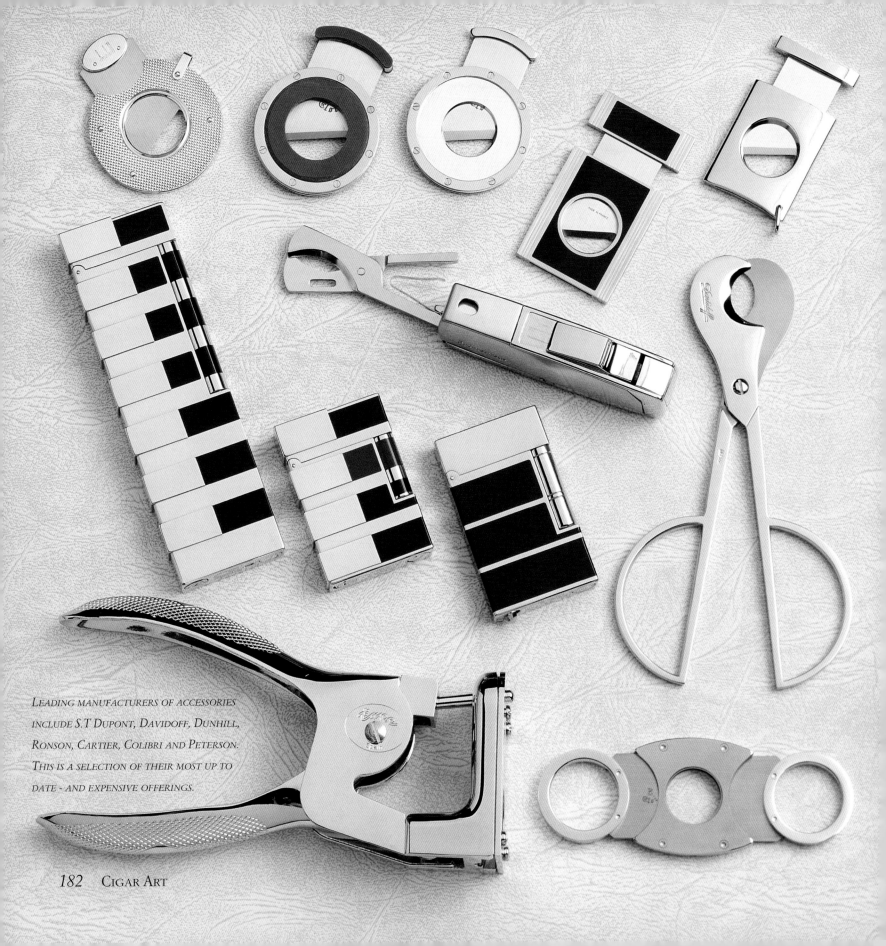

LEADING MANUFACTURERS OF ACCESSORIES
INCLUDE S.T DUPONT, DAVIDOFF, DUNHILL,
RONSON, CARTIER, COLIBRI AND PETERSON.
THIS IS A SELECTION OF THEIR MOST UP TO
DATE - AND EXPENSIVE OFFERINGS.

Above A COHIBA ACCESSORIES RANGE WITH LEATHER WALLETS, KEY RINGS AND A YELLOW AND BLACK CIGAR CASE DESIGNED FOR THE COHIBA SIGLO 6, WHICH IS A HEAVY RING GAUGE CIGAR.

Above 'DARLINGS' COLLECTION ASHTRAY DESIGNED BY ENZINA FUSCHINI AND MADE BY LIMOGES, MAKERS OF THE WHITEST PORCELAIN IN THE WORLD. THE IDEA OF THESE BLACK AND WHITE FIGURES AT A COCKTAIL PARTY WAS PART OF A DESIGN THEME FOR A 'BLACK AND WHITE' CHARITY BALL.

Left and above FOR WOMEN CIGAR LOVERS: THESE HANDBAGS ARE MADE OUT OF OLD CIGAR BOXES AND COME WITH A VARIETY OF LININGS.

Above DRAWER WITH VARIOUS ACCESSORIES, ASHTRAYS, LIGHTERS AND TWO SUEDE LINED AREAS FOR A CUTTER AND A LIGHTER.

THE WORSHIPFUL COMPANY OF FURNITURE MAKERS IN LONDON AWARDS A GUILD MARK TO THE MAKER OF FURNITURE WHICH IS EXCEPTIONAL IN DESIGN AND CRAFTSMANSHIP. THIS ROMEO Y JULIETA HUMIDOR BY MARTIN LANE WAS AWARDED GUILD MARK NO. 353. BELOW: A SANDBLASTED ROMEO Y JULIETA LOGO DECORATES THE TOP.

Right THERE ARE EIGHT DOVETAILED DRAWERS WITH SOLID, RIPPLED SYCAMORE FRONTS. IN THE CENTRE OF EACH IS A BEVELLED GLASS PANEL ENGRAVED WITH A LEAF. *Opposite* ANOTHER EXTRAORDINARY HUMIDOR BY MARTIN LANE TO COMMEMORATE THE 150TH ANNIVERSARY OF HARRODS, LONDON. AWARDED GUILD MARK NO. 286.

CIGAR
People

༄

HERE is a fascinating, anecdotal who's who of Anwer Bati's favourite famous cigar smokers, ranging from politicians to Hollywood film stars. The image of cigars has been greatly influenced by the people who smoke them and by the occasions on which they are smoked.

ADAMS, JOHN QUINCY

Sixth President (1825-29) of the United States, was a cigar lover. He accompanied his father, John Adams (later 2nd President), to Europe as a child, and was partly educated there. Later, as a diplomat, he almost certainly acquired his love of cigars during his travels. In 1814, he negotiated the Treaty of Ghent, which ended the War of 1812 between Britain and the United States. An important member of his negotiating team was none other than Henry Clay – see below – after whom one of the most famous of cigar brands was named.

BARTHELEMY, AUGUSTE

The French 19th century poet wrote a *Manual on the Art of Smoking* – in 5,000 verses including: *For the man who is not a hapless layman, 'neath the firmament nothing surpasses the Havana cigar.*
The sun that browns it swells with pride.

And he offered the advice:

'It is necessary to know how to smoke so that one knows how to choose.

The true smoker abstains from imitating Vesuvius.

He demonstrates the requirement that during three-quarters of an hour

A cigar rests in his hand without going out.'

BERLE, MILTON

The one-time Milton Berlinger was originally a vaudevillian,

radio comedian, and occasional film actor. His fondness for fine cigars was combined with considerable knowledge. He stocked up on Dunhills, Upmanns and Davidoffs when the American embargo on Cuba was announced, and later favoured Dominican Davidoffs, though he once said: "I'd rather smoke a *figurado*, Montecristo No. 2, than any cigar. I love its shape."

BISMARCK, OTTO VON

The 19th century German statesman and 'Iron Chancellor' was a keen smoker of cigars and one of the personalities of his age who helped to make cigars fashionable. Legend has it that once, riding down the *Bois de Boulogne* in Paris after the French surrender following the Franco-Prussian war of 1870, Bismarck sensed hostility from the Parisians around him. However, he soon diffused a potentially dangerous situation by asking a passer-by for a light for his cigar. On another occasion, it is said that he gave his last cigar to a dying soldier, and commented: "I have never enjoyed a cigar so much as that one I never smoked."

Above OTTO VON BISMARCK, MOUNTED RIGHT.

BOCK, GUSTAVO (or GUSTAVE)

The Dutchman (though some say he was German) credited with inventing the cigar band in the 19th century. The date for this innovation has usually been given as 1850, but this is probably incorrect. The evidence comes from Bock's 1904 publication *La Verdad Sobre la Industria del tabaco Habano* (*The Truth About the Havana Manufacturing Industry*), written when he was director of Buck Duke's Tobacco Trust. In it he says: 'Having, during a residence on this island of 46 years, devoted all my time to discovering, in the minutest detail, the best methods for the production of the highest-quality of Havana cigars...' – which would suggest he didn't get to Cuba until 1858. He was one of the first Europeans to own a Cuban tobacco plantation, and was responsible for brands such as El Aguila de Oro, La Flor de Henry Clay and Lords of England, all of which carried his name. He also wrote *The Art of Smoking the Cigar*.

BONAPARTE, NAPOLEON III

The nephew of Napoleon Bonaparte himself, when Emperor of France (1852-70), was asked to ban smoking. His reply: "This vice brings in a hundred million a year in taxes. I shall certainly ban it at once – as soon as you can name a virtue that raises as much money." He was a keen cigar smoker who was once given a gift of 20,000 Havanas, carrying his monogram.

BURNS, GEORGE

The great American comic, who died in 1996, aged over 100, was rarely seen without a cigar in his mouth. He was paid to promote the cheap American El Producto brand, justifying it by saying that more expensive cigars went out too often to be useable in his stage act. Asked what his doctor thought of his cigar smoking, he replied: "I don't know, my doctor's dead."

BYRON, LORD

One of the most celebrated literary figures of the 19th Century, ended his ode *Sublime Tobacco*, in *The Island*, with the lines:

Yet thy true lovers more adore by far
Thy naked beauties – Give me a cigar!

A Cuban brand was named after him, and another, La Poeta, featured him among portraits of great writers on its label.

CAINE, SIR MICHAEL

The British film star, who was recently knighted, has been a hand-made cigar smoker ever since he found fame in the 1960s with the films *Zulu* and *Alfie*. He buys his cigars in London, in boxes of 50, containing a selection of 10 each of Montecristo sizes 1-5.

He has been known to refer to it as "a box of allsorts."

CARUSO, ENRICO

Originally named Errico, the great Naples-born opera singer, died aged only 48 in 1921, and was so fond of Havanas that he had a clause in his contracts demanding *'the right to smoke on any part of the stage from the moment the curtain rises.'*

CASTRO, FIDEL

The Cuban leader, who overthrew General Fulgencio Batista in 1959, was a keen smoker, who was often pictured holding or smoking a cigar. When in 1955 he was held prisoner on the island of Pines, his followers sent him messages rolled into cigars. One CIA plot, among many, to get rid of him involved tampering with his cigars. But he stopped smoking many years ago, in theory to discourage his fellow countrymen from smoking. Even so, Castro's signature seems to sell cigars. From 1993 to 1997 cigar boxes signed by him raised around a million dollars, and his presence at auctions also seems to do wonders.

CHURCHILL, SIR WINSTON

There couldn't be a more famous or dedicated cigar smoker than great British war leader. He once said: "I always carry Cuba in my mouth." He preferred big cigars (often double coronas) with dark wrappers – though he would usually only smoke them half way through. And he is one of the few people to have had a cigar size named after him, originally by Romeo y Julieta, but also by many other brands. The standard Churchill size is 7 inches x 47 ring gauge, but many cigars bearing his name come in slightly different sizes.

He lived until he was 91, and is thought to have smoked more than 200,000 cigars during his long life. Many of them were supplied to him free by companies such as Jamaica Tobacco Co, and Hoyo de Monterrey, then owned by Palicio. But Churchill had regular struggles with British Customs and Excise to keep the cigars given to him without paying duty on them.

Churchill developed his love for Havanas when he went (as a reporter for *The Daily Graphic*) to Cuba in 1895 during the Spanish-American war. He later bought his supplies from Robert Lewis, the great London cigar merchant, as well as from Dunhill. The shop's records show that his first order was placed in 1900, and the last a month before he died in 1965.

During the Blitz, after a German bomb hit the Dunhill shop, a stressed-out manager telephoned at 2 am to give the vital message, "Your cigars are safe, sir." Churchill's favoured cigars during the war were actually El Trovator, made in Jamaica. This is because foreign exchange restrictions prevented cigars being imported from Cuba. Nearby Jamaica, a British colony, was inside the Sterling area, so Anglo-Cuban factories were set up there. They used a mixture of local and Cuban tobacco, and Havana wrappers. El Trovator was one of these cigars.

In his seven-volume official biography of Churchill, Martin Gilbert quotes a minister who, with his colleagues, met the great man in the underground Cabinet bunker one day in 1941. "I have something to show you," said Churchill, pointing to a large imitation Queen Anne-style cabinet with the inscription 'To the Rt. Hon. Winston Churchill, PC, MP, Prime Minister of Great Britain. A tribute of admiration from the President and People of Cuba.'

Churchill then said: "I have had some difficulty today in getting this through the Customs." Then, opening one of the drawers of Havanas, he turned to his ministers, saying: "Gentlemen, I am now going to try an experiment. Maybe it will result in joy. Maybe it will end in grief. I am about to give you each one of these magnificent cigars." Then he paused, and said: "It may well be that each of these contain some deadly poison." The minister also recalled some days after this event that the cigars were indeed tested for poison.

When hosting a lunch for the King of Saudi Arabia (Ibn Saud), he asked an interpreter to say, "that if it was the religion of His Majesty to deprive himself of smoking and alcohol I must point

Right SIR WINSTON CHURCHILL.

out that my rule of life prescribed as an absolutely sacred rite smoking of cigars and also the drinking of alcohol before, after, and if need be during all meals and in the intervals between them."

Churchill's daughter, Lady Soames, inherited a love of cigars from her father. In his controversial diaries, Lord Wyatt records that, one evening: 'Mary smoked a cigar after dinner. Quite a big one. She said Papa didn't smoke as many cigars as people thought.' It was, indeed claimed in a book published in the late 1990s, that in the last 15 years of his life, Churchill only really flourished cigars for photographers. On public occasions during the war, and afterwards, Churchill used to cradle his cigars between his index and middle fingers, displaying his famous 'V' sign. But in private, there is photographic evidence that he held them more conventionally – between index finger and thumb.

One of the most memorable photographs of Winston Churchill, Yousuf Karsh's 1941 portrait, shows him without his customary cigar. Churchill, looking his most defiant, was actually deprived of it by Karsh, who recalled: 'Churchill's cigar was ever present. I held out an ashtray, but he would not dispose of it... Then I stepped towards him and, without premeditation, but ever so respectfully, I said, "Forgive me, sir" and plucked the cigar from his mouth. By the time I got back to my camera, he looked so belligerent he could have devoured me.'

CIFUENTES

This great Cuban cigar-making family, one of those that fled Cuba after the Revolution, owned the Partagas factory from 1920, and other brands such as Ramon Allones.Ramon Cifuentes (whose father, also called Ramon, was instrumental in making Partagas a great marque) was originally responsible for creating Dominican-made Partagas (in 1978), eventually owned by General Cigar. There is a Dominican brand called Cifuentes.

CLAY, HENRY

The 19th century lawyer, farmer, and statesman (1777-1852) was one of the best known American political figures of his time. He was noted for his quick wit, and as a hard drinker, gambler, and lover of cigars. One of the most famous Cuban brands of the 19th Century, now made in the Dominican Republic, was named after him.

CLINTON, WILLIAM JEFFERSON

It's difficult to be quite certain if Bill Clinton (born William Jefferson Blythe IV), 42nd President of the United States, still smokes cigars. His wife, Hilary Rodham Clinton banned smoking at the White House, but it is rumoured that, for instance, he surreptitiously enjoyed a Macanudo Portofino while his wife was away at a women's conference in Beijing; and that he smoked a cigar with his National Security Adviser, Anthony Lake, to celebrate the rescue of airman Scott O'Grady in Bosnia, in 1995. Only the second U.S. President to have to face impeachment hearings (in 1999), he is notoriously associated with one of the most famous cigars in history – not smoked as far as we know – during his relationship with White House intern Monica Lewinsky. The cigar was supposedly given to him by Palestinian leader Yasser Arafat.

COLETTE, SIDONIE-GABRIELLE

The French novelist, who died in Paris in 1954 once observed: "When a wife can purchase her husband the right cigars, their relationship is blessed." In her 1944 novel *Gigi* (later made into a stage musical and a film), Aunt Alice says: "Let me think how I will teach you to choose cigars... when a woman knows a man's preferences, cigars included, and when a man knows what pleases a woman, they are well armed for life together."

COPPOLA, FRANCIS FORD

The director of such memorable films as *Apocalypse Now*, *The Godfather* trilogy, *The Cotton Club* and Bram Stoker's *Dracula*, is a devoted cigar smoker. It's a habit he inherited from his father Carmine (who liked Italian cigars such as Toscani). He owns a gold and silver cigar cutter, which once belonged to the studio boss Jack Warner – who taught him how to light a cigar properly. He is also an enthusiastic and successful wine producer, with vineyards in California's Napa Valley.

DAVIDOFF, ZINO

Russian born (in 1906), and one of the greatest names in the cigar world. His father had a tobacco shop in Kiev, and Zino followed him into the business after the family moved to Switzerland in 1912. He spent two years in Cuba during the 1920s, learning about all aspects of tobacco cultivation and cigar making, and developed his love of Havanas, under the tutelage of the Palicio family. In 1945, he developed his Chateau series in cooperation with the Hoyo de Monterrey factory (then owned by the Palicios). And, after World War II, he established himself as perhaps the world's greatest cigar merchant. In 1969, he had a Havana brand (made in the El Laguito factory) with its distinctive white and gold band, named after him. Davidoff – his business was owned by the Swiss company Oettinger by this time – fell out with the Cubans in the 1980s, and cigars bearing his name now come from the Dominican Republic, where they have been made since 1990. In 1983, Davidoff introduced the, Honduras-made Zino brand to the United States. But Cuban Davidoffs continue to fetch very high prices. He once said: "I was working with Cuba for 60 years. Cuba was like a nice lady, but it was time for a change. I have found a new lady, younger, thinner, lighter, so I have made a new marriage." The Davidoff shops, established around the world (the main one is in Geneva, the others are mostly franchised) as a result of Oetttinger's takeover, are stylish temples to smoking, selling many elegant accessories as well as cigars. Davidoff, who died in 1994, wrote two books on cigars and cigar smoking (the last being *The Connoisseur's Book of the Cigar*), both originally published in French. 'A well-chosen cigar is like armour and is useful against the torments of life. A little blue smoke mysteriously removes anxiety,' he observed.

DENIRO, ROBERT

The movie star not only likes cigars, but has also smoked them in films such as Martin Scosese's *Cape Fear* (1991) in which he played the evil Max Cady. The cigars were fat, but cheap. Playing a New York detective, he also smokes throughout the movie *15 Minutes* (2001), until he meets his untimely death.

DUFY, RAOUL

The French painter and designer (1877-1953) was a dedicated cigar smoker, who sometimes bartered his pictures for cigars.

DUKE, JAMES B. – See pages 28-29.

DUNHILL, ALFRED

This old English company (originally a saddle and harness business) has had a long association with fine cigars. Alfred Dunhill's original London tobacco shop opened in 1907, and he was one of the first cigar merchants to use walk-in humidors. The Dunhill shops in London and New York were to become among the most famous in the world. Dunhill also had a shop in Paris. It was to Dunhill that the Menendez y Garcia company first took their infant Montecristo brand in 1935. And the firm also developed house brands such as Don Candido and Don Alfredo. The 1980s saw the brief appearance of Dunhill's own brand of Havanas, sporting a red band bearing the company's elongated 'd' logo on cigars with names such as Cabinetta, Malecon and Mojito. Cuban production stopped in 1989. Dunhill hand-made cigars now come from the Dominican Republic, Honduras and the Canary Islands. You might still find some Cuban Dunhills at auction – selling for very high prices. Alfred Dunhill wrote a book, *The Gentle Art of Smoking*.

EDWARD VII, KING OF ENGLAND

A noted cigar lover, preferring double coronas, which bore q personalized band featuring the Prince of Wales' ostrich plumes. There is a Romeo y Julieta named after him, as is the American mass-market machine-made brand, King Edward. He apparently liked to pierce his cigars, rather than cut them. His grandson, Edward VIII, was celebrated by the La Corona brand's commemorative labels for the British market, featuring a portrait of Edward in naval uniform, and images of Windsor Castle and St. James's Palace. An earlier label from the same brand shows his parents, George V and Queen Mary.

ELGAR, SIR EDWARD

The great British composer wrote his *Enigma Variations* after his wife suggested that he smoke a cigar. He went to his piano, and the main theme started to emerge.

FAROUK I, KING OF EGYPT

The ill-fated playboy king reigned from 1936 until 1952. He was an enthusiastic smoker of big cigars, notably double coronas. The aptly named Visible Inmeso cigar, (18 in long x 47 ring gauge) was specially made for him. He used to buy 5,000 cigars a time, and was supposed to have ordered 40,000 Hoyo de Monterrey double coronas from the Davidoff shop in Geneva.

FOCH, MARSHAL FERDINAND

The French hero of the First World War found that cigars helped him to concentrate, particularly when he had a big military decision to make.

FREUD, SIGMUND

The Viennese founder of psychoanalysis, who died in 1939, was a habitual cigar smoker and started at the age of 24. He often used to smoke during his consultations, and shortly before his death, he said: "I owe to the cigar a great intensification of my capacity to work and a facilitation of my self-control". Though presumably followers of his theory can make other judgements about the unconscious symbolism of his cigar smoking.

Right SIGMUND FREUD.

FROST, SIR DAVID

The transatlantic talk show host, TV interviewer (his most important interview was with former U.S. President Richard Nixon), and media entrepreneur, has rarely been far from a cigar since he first came to fame with the British TV show *That Was the Week That Was* in the 1960s. When they were available, his cigars of choice were large Cuban-made Davidoffs.

GRANT, ULYSSES S.

The American Civil War commander of the Union armies and eventual 18th President (1869-77) of the United States used to smoke ten cigars a day, but this number went up to as many as 25 cigars, particularly after he received thousands as gifts from admirers. He was only 46 when he became President, and his campaign song was *A Smokin' His Cigar*. Photographed by Matthew Brady smoking, he was also friendly with cigar fanatic Mark Twain – see below. One of the great cigar what-might-have-beens of history is the fact that during his time as President, he advocated the annexation of the Dominican Republic, a move narrowly rejected by the Senate.

GUEVARA, CHE (ERNESTO GUEVARA DE LA SERNA)

The Argentine-born revolutionary and left-wing cult hero was for a while Cuba's minister of industry. He met his end in 1967 at the hands of government troops in Bolivia. He

Above CHE GUEVARA.

once wrote: 'An habitual and extremely important complement in the life of a guerrilla is smoking ...for the smoke that he can expel in moments of relaxation is a great companion to the lonely soldier.' When Cohiba was first launched internationally, it was rumoured (cynics suggest for marketing purposes) that Che had been responsible for the brand. But this was a myth: he had already been in Bolivia for a year when it was founded.

HEMINGWAY, ERNEST

The great American novelist lived in Cuba for 30 years, until his death in 1961. His house, not far outside Havana, is still preserved as a museum. The legendary drinker was associated with many bars around the world, but perhaps his favourite was El Floridita, in the heart of the former financial district of Old Havana. He was as keen on cigars as he was on drinking, bullfights, sea-fishing and big game hunting. A number of his novels and short stories use Cuban locations, and he mentions cigars in novels such as *The Old Man of the Sea* and *The Sun also Rises*. In the latter, one character, the Count, says: 'I like a cigar to really draw... Half the cigars you smoke don't draw.'

HITCHCOCK, SIR ALFRED

The great British film director, who died in 1980, aged 81, and directed the first successful British 'talkie', *Blackmail* (1929), as well as his later legendary suspense dramas, was a keen cigar smoker both on the set and off. A number of his films include scenes involving cigars. The 1966 Cold War thriller, *Torn Curtain*, for instance, contains a scene in which an East German security man offers Paul Newman (a real life cigar smoker) a cigar with the line: "Cuban – your loss, our gain." Although cigars are normally associated with power, in his 1946 film *Notorious*, Hitchcock depicted a wealthy Nazi sympathiser not only smoking cigars, but also referring to a shipment of Havanas he is expecting. The character is weak, dominated by his mother, and his love of cigars suggests a soft, pampered existence – in contrast to the tough, cigarette-smoking American secret agent played by Cary Grant.

HOOD, THOMAS
In 1840, the British poet, known for his humorous and socially concerned verses, wrote *The Cigar*:

Some sigh for this and that;
My wishes don't go far;
The world may wag at will,
So I have my cigar.

HUSSEIN, SADDAM
The former Iraqi dictator, who was deposed in the 2003 Iraq War, and captured some months later, was a keen smoker of Havana cigars. He was amply supplied with gifts of cigars by the Cuban government, and visiting officials from other communist regimes, particularly when his country was within the Soviet sphere of influence. His deputy, the suave Tariq Aziz, was equally fond of cigars.

INFANTE, GUILLERMO CABRERA
The Cuban novelist and diplomat wrote a famous book of vignettes featuring cigars, *Holy Smoke* (1985).

KENNEDY, JOHN F.
Although President John .F Kennedy, a regular cigar smoker, imposed the full American embargo on Cuba (there was already a partial one), it wasn't until he had acquired a decent stock of cigars for himself. One evening, in February 1962, some months after the Bay of Pigs incident, Kennedy summoned his Press Secretary, and fellow cigar lover, Pierre Salinger, and asked him to find 1,000 Petit Upmanns by the following morning. At 8 am the next day, an anxious Kennedy called him in again, and after being told that Salinger had

Above JOHN F. KENNEDY.

managed to find as many as 1,200 cigars, immediately took out a pen and signed the decree banning all Cuban products from the United States. Shown below are examples of the brands that Kennedy favoured; however he would not have smoked these as they are machine-made.

A few months after the embargo was imposed, Salinger (whose own favourite is Partagas Lusitania) was in Moscow for talks with Khrushchev. The Soviet leader, who didn't like cigars, gave him a case of 250 Havanas. Knowing

he would be breaking the embargo, Salinger decided he would, nonetheless, take them back to the United States, taking advantage of his diplomatic passport. When he reported back to Kennedy, with whom he had intended to share the cigars, the President, fearful of a scandal, immediately ordered him to declare them to U.S. Customs so that they could be destroyed. Salinger did his duty but, to this day, suspects that the customs officers almost certainly took pleasure in destroying them one by one.

William Stryon, the American Pulitzer Prize-winning novelist, author of *Sophie's Choice* (1979) recalled an evening with Kennedy in the early 1960s. After dinner, Kennedy passed around tubed Cuban Partagas to his guests, even though this was well after the embargo. Styron decided to keep his as a souvenir, and instead lit up one of his own Canary Island cigars. The following November he met Kennedy, who was smoking a cigar, at a party in New York. JFK's parting words were: "Take care." Two weeks later, he was assassinated. On that day, Styron smoked his Partagas in memory of the slain President.

KIPLING, RUDYARD

The Nobel Prize-winning poet, author of *Gunga Din*, and other works celebrating the British Empire, was a cigar lover who (in *The Betrothed*) wrote the notorious line, *A woman is only a woman, but a good cigar is a smoke*. The comment has been widely misunderstood, because taken out of context. The poem (1886) is satirical, about choosing between a woman, Maggie, and smoking, and was inspired by a breach of promise case brought in 1885, during which it was alleged that a husband preferred his cigars to his wife. Kipling was merely trying to enter the mind of the husband in the case. *The Betrothed* mentions a number of Havana brands such as Larranaga, Partagas and Henry Clay, and demonstrates a considerable knowledge of cigars. To quote a few lines:

Open the old cigar box, get me a Cuba stout,
For things are running crossways, and Maggie and I are out.

We quarrelled about Havanas – we fought o'er a good cheroot,
And I know she is exacting, and she says I am a brute.....

There's peace in a Larranaga, there's calm in a Henry Clay.
But the best cigar in an hour is finished and thrown away -

Open the old cigar-box – let me consider a while.
Here is a mild Manilla – there is a wifely smile....

Which is the better portion – bondage bought with a ring,
Or a harem of dusky beauties, fifty tied in a string?...

A million surplus Maggies are willing to bear the yoke;
And a woman is only a woman, but a good cigar is a Smoke

Light me another Cuba – I hold to my first-sworn vows.
If Maggie will have no rival, I will have no Maggie for Spouse!

LA ROCHEFOUCAULD, DUC DE

The 18th century French diplomat (descendant of La Rochefoucauld, author of the Maxims), who was sent to liase with the American revolutionary government in 1794, wrote of his voyage: 'The cigar is a great resource. It is necessary to have travelled for a long time on a ship to understand that at least the cigar affords you the pleasure of smoking. It raises your spirits. Are you troubled by something? The cigar will dissolve it... Are you harassed by unpleasant thoughts? Smoking a cigar puts one in a frame of mind to dispense with these... If you are obsessed by sad thoughts, a cigar will take your mind off them...Sometimes they die out, and happy are those who do not need to relight too quickly'. This may be the earliest published French reference to cigars.

LENIN, VLADIMIR ILYICH

The Russian revolutionary, and future Soviet leader, apparently used to buy cigars from Henri Davidoff's shop in Geneva. Zino Davidoff, his son, recorded that Vladimir Ulyanov, as he was born, never paid his bill. However, he had adopted the pseudonym Lenin in 1901, much earlier than his time in Switzerland – just before, and during the First World War- so it may be a tall tale. But Davidoff, who can have been no more than a child at the time, later said of the revolutionaries he met: 'One of them greatly impressed me. He had a thin face and brilliant eyes and spoke in a loud voice. He also took cigars and didn't pay for them. My father never tried to recover the money. On a bill that I have kept as a souvenir are stamped the words 'Not Paid' and the name of this customer – Vladimir Ulyanov.'

LISZT, FRANZ

The composer was an inveterate smoker who always carried a large wooden case of cigars. He once said: "A good Cuban cigar closes the door to the vulgarities of the world."

LONSDALE, LORD

The British aristocrat and great cigar lover was one of the few people to give his name to a cigar size, created for him. It is now one of the most popular sizes available (usually 6 in x 42 ring gauge). The Rafael Gonzalez brand used to carry his portrait on the inside of the box lid.

MALLARMÉ, STEPHANE

The French 19th century poet was introduced to cigars by his father. He once wrote: 'What voluptuousness when I lunched with my father... After finishing the meal he produced boxes of sparkling cigars: Valle, Clay, Upmann. I opened these boxes which evoked visions of dancing girls, and I removed the bands, because that is what is to be done...". He was painted with a cigar in his hand by both Edourd Manet and Francois Nardi.

MANN, THOMAS

The German author of *Buddenbrooks* and *The Magic Mountain*. Mann has a character (Hans Castort) in the latter book saying: 'I fail to understand how one can live without smoking. It means, undoubtedly, depriving oneself of the best part of existence and, in any case, a very considerable pleasure...'.

MARTI, JOSE

The Cuban revolutionary, noted for his poems and essays, unified and led the revolt against Spain in 1895. He died, fighting, the same year (aged only 42) but Cuban independence was achieved seven years later. His campaign was largely funded by exiled Cuban tobacco workers, and given dynamism by the increasingly politicised Cuban industrial working class, led by the cigar workers. News of his landing was sent to his supporters from Key West, concealed in a cigar. One of the main Havana factories (formerly H. Upmann) is named after him. He once wrote of tobacco that it was the 'comfort of the pensive, delight of the daydreamer…'. Although there isn't a Havana brand named after him, brands from both the Dominican Republic and Nicaragua have borne his name.

Above José Martí.

MARX, GROUCHO

A legendary cigar smoker. Once, when his wife asked him to give up cigars, he said, "No, but we can remain good friends." On another occasion, a woman told him she had 22 children because she loved her husband. He replied: " I like my cigar, too. But I take it out of my mouth once in a while." And, he said: "A thing that has always baffled me about women is that they will saturate themselves with a pint of perfume, a pound of sachet powder, an evil-smelling hair ointment and a half-dozen varieties of body oils, and then have the effrontery to complain about the aroma of a fine cigar." He liked his cigars strong. A particular favourite was the Dunhill 410.

MARX, KARL

Born in Prussia (1818), Marx moved to London in 1849, and died there in 1883. He was very fond of cigars. One day, in Holborn, he saw a tobacconist's window advertising cheap cigars with the slogan: 'The more you smoke, the more you save.' He demonstrated his understanding of economics by telling his friends that he would save one shilling and sixpence per box if he bought them, and that if he smoked enough of them, he might one day be able to live on his "savings". But, as Francis Wheen wrote in his acclaimed 1999 biography, 'the theory was tested with such lung-rasping commitment that eventually the family doctor had to intervene, ordering the wheezing patient to find some other way of enriching himself.'

MAUGHAM, (WILLIAM) SOMERSET

The richest writer in the world for a time, his autobiography tells of his love for cigars: 'A good cigar is one of the best pleasures that I know. At the time when I was young and very poor, I only smoked cigars, which were offered to me. I promised myself that if I ever had some money that I would savour a cigar each day after lunch and after dinner. This is the only resolution of my youth that I have kept, and the only realized ambition, which has not brought disillusion. I like a mild cigar, of delicate aroma and medium length. If the cigar is too small, you can not enjoy the smoke. If too fat, the smoke overwhelms you.'

MENCKEN, HENRY LOUIS

The great Baltimore born and based American wit, journalist and critic (1880-1956) had cigars in his blood: he was the son of a cigar factory owner of German stock, August Mencken. He worked in his father's factory when he was young, before setting out to be one of America's most celebrated journalists and commentators. He hated the cigar business, but loved cigars (having even learned to roll them), which he started smoking aged 16. He ordered 300 cigars a month, but often couldn't smoke them fully thanks to bouts of hay fever. When a group of women called for cigars to be banned on Baltimore's trams, he wrote: 'Women, in general, are not nearly so delicate as romance makes them. A woman who can stand half an hour of the Lexington fish market is well able to face a few blasts of tobacco smoke.' He also said, "Not one in 10,000 [women] can tell the difference between good tobacco and bad."

MENENDEZ

One of the great Cuban cigar families, who owned H. Upmann and Montecristo, with the Garcias. The family, led by Alonzo Menendez, who had come from Spain in 1890, left Cuba after the revolution to make Montecruz cigars in the Canary Islands. Later, Alonzo's son, Benjamin Menendez, oversaw the production of General Cigar's brands (including Partagas, Temple Hall and Macanudo) made in Jamaica and in the Dominican

Republic. He said: 'A cigar always has its own time of day. The milder the taste, the more it can be enjoyed in the morning. The fuller the body, the more it belongs in the evening.' His own favourite is the (Dominican) Partagas Limited Reserve Royale (6¾ in x 43 ring gauge), which he finds strong, mellow, and 'an exceptional after-dinner cigar.'

MUSSET, ALFRED DE

The 19th century French poet, novelist and playwright was a dedicated cigar smoker. He called the cigar 'The best way of killing time.' He also wrote, 'Any cigar smoker is a friend, because I know what he feels.' Among his cigar-smoking friends were Franz Liszt and George Sand, about whom he wrote a poem describing her smoking a cigar.

NICHOLSON, JACK

The movie star started smoking cigars thanks to his role as the petty officer in *The Last Detail* (1973). The experience made him start smoking again – he had earlier kicked cigarettes.

PALICIO

The family owned Hoyo de Monterrey and Punch before the Cuban Revolution. The Punch brand is most closely associated with Fernando Palicio, its last private owner, who also owned the Belinda brand. He was important in popularising the half corona size (Petit Punch), particularly in Britain. The Palicios also created the Macanudo brand, an offshoot of Punch, which started production in Jamaica during World War II, thus allowing the

cigars to come within the Sterling area, and allowing them to be exported to Britain. The Palicios also helped the young Zino Davidoff to learn his trade, and produced his Chateau series of cigars in Cuba. The trademarks for non-Cuban Hoyo de Monterrey and Punch passed to Villazon (now a subsidiary of General Cigar), headed by Cuban exile Frank Llaneza. They are made in Honduras.

PUTNAM, ISRAEL

The man credited with introducing cigars to North America in 1762. Colonel Israel Putnam had been an officer in the British army and took part in the siege and six-month British occupation of Havana – where he discovered cigars. In 1775, Putnam gained another claim to fame by being appointed a major general in the Continental Army and fighting with distinction against the British at Bunker Hill in the American War of Independence. He died in 1790.

RAVEL, MAURICE

The French composer (1875-1937), perhaps best known for the *Bolero*, came from a prosperous background (his father was Swiss, his mother a Basque). Although he was a reclusive character, he was a serious Havana smoker, who said smoking helped him to compose his orchestral works and those for piano. Fellow cigar lover Collete was the librettist for his best-known opera *The Child and the Enchantments* (1925).

ROTHSCHILD

Members of the great banking family have long been cigar connoisseurs, particularly the wine producers of the French branch. They allowed the name of some of their greatest wines to be used by Zino Davidoff for his Chateau series of cigars. Later, when the Zino Mouton Cadet series was launched in the 1980s, Baroness Phillipine de Rothschild accompanied Davidoff on a promotional tour of the United States. Rothschild is the name sometimes given to the robusto size of non-Cuban cigars. It was created for a member of the British branch of the family, the 2nd Lord Rothschild.

RUBINSTEIN, ARTUR

The great Polish-born pianist, who gave his first public recital in Berlin, aged 13, loved cigars. He commanded huge fees, and used some of them to buy a plantation in the Vuelta Abajo region of Cuba before the revolution. He also had the foresight to secure enough Havanas for the rest of his life shortly before the revolution. His favourite brand was Romeo y Julieta, though his cigars carried personalised bands with his face on them.

Above ROMEO Y JULIETA BOX LITHOGRAPH.

SAND, GEORGE

The French 19th century novelist often smoked cigars. Before she became an established writer, Sand used to supplement her income by embellishing cigar boxes with water colour designs. She once wrote, 'Cigars calm pain and people loneliness with a thousand gracious images.' In 1845, when she lit up a large cigar in front of a young Russian aristocrat, she responded to his obvious amazement by saying, "In St.Petersburg I probably would not be able to smoke a cigar in a salon." To which he supposedly replied: " In no salon, Madame, have I ever seen a woman smoking a cigar." A women-only cigar society in Santa Monica, California was named after her.

SCHWARZENEGGER, ARNOLD

Now Governor of California, Schwarzenegger is a shrewd businessman, as well as remaining one of the biggest box office names in Hollywood. The Austrian-born former body-builder is married to TV presenter Maria Shriver, a member of the Kennedy family, and it was her father, Sargent Shriver, who first introduced him to 'real' cigars at the Kennedy compound in Hyannisport in 1977. His favourite is the Cohiba Esplendido, though he also smokes other brands, such as Davidoff, from time to time. He wielded a cigar in the 1986 film *Raw Deal*.

SCOTT, RIDLEY

The British director of films such as *Blade Runner*, *Alien* and *Gladiator*, originally trained as a designer, and is famed for his visual flair. As the man who made 1492, the epic film (starring Gerard Depardieu) about Columbus' momentous voyage, it is fitting that he likes Cuban cigars, Cohibas in particular. His brother Tony Scott, who directed such high-octane movies as *Top Gun*, is also a cigar lover. In *Crimson Tide*, Gene Hackman (playing a

submarine commander) offers a cigar to his subordinate (played by Denzel Washington) with the remark: "Your last taste of polluted air for the next 65 days. I don't trust air I can't see."

SIBELIUS, JEAN

The great Finnish composer, creator of seven symphonies, once wrote in thanks for a gift of Cuban cigars sent to him on his 83rd birthday: 'Since one of my uncles lived and died in Cuba, I have always been greatly interested in your admirable country. Moreover, I have smoked Havana cigars all my life and, of course, they have always been highly meaningful for me.'

SINATRA, FRANK

'Ol Blue Eyes', who died in 1998, liked the Lonsdale size: particularly the Saint Luis Rey, and the Montecristo No1. Apart from smoking cigars in the company of his 'Rat Pack', and John F. Kennedy, he also smoked with his friends in the Mafia – not least in their hotels and casinos in Havana.

STENDHAL

The French early 19th century author of *The Red and the Black* (1830) and *The Charterhouse of Parma* (1839), often mentioned cigars in his work. He especially liked Italian Toscani cigars, and wrote 'On a cold morning in winter, a Toscani cigar fortifies the soul.'

THACKERAY, WILLIAM MAKEPEACE

The 19th century English novelist wrote: 'Honest men, with pipes and cigars in their mouths, have great physical advantages in conversation...the

cigar harmonises the society, and soothes at once the speaker and the subject whereon he converses... I vow and believe that the cigar has been one of the greatest creature-comforts of my life – a kind companion, a gentle stimulant, an amiable anodyne, a cementer of friendship.'

TROLLOPE, ANTHONY

The Victorian civil servant and novelist very much enjoyed smoking cigars himself (a photograph of him smoking exists) but his wife, Rose, forced him to do so in the garden.

TWAIN, MARK

The great American humourist and author couldn't have been a more dedicated cigar smoker. He used to smoke around ten cheap cigars a day, but many more if he was in the middle of writing a book. He also liked more expensive ones, from time to time, sometimes with his friend and fellow cigar lover, President Ulysses Grant. On one occasion, he described his smoking habits during the five hours a day during which he wrote: 'I smoke with all my might, and allow no intervals." He once tried to cut down: 'I pledged myself to smoke but one cigar a day... But desire persecuted me every day and all day

long. I found myself hunting for larger cigars... within the month my cigar had grown to such proportions I could have used it as a crutch.'

VAN DONGEN, KEES

The Fauvist Dutch painter who died in 1968 in Monaco, once wrote, 'The cigar, like the pipe, ought to match your physique.' It's good advice.

WAGNER, RICHARD

The great German operatic composer once told some Viennese admirers who had given him a gift of cigars: 'You have unquestionably helped in my opera *Die Gotterdammerung*. This morning these marvels from Havana arrived and they immediately transported me to such enchantment as Pythia must have felt when she was enveloped in the vapours of Apollo.'

Above PORTRAIT OF WAGNER ON A 'FLOR DE WAGNER' BOX LABEL.

WARNER, JACK

Living up to the image of a movie producer, the great Hollywood studio boss, who with his three brothers founded Warner Brothers in 1923, was a famed smoker. He preferred mild, pale cigars. Once, he won 100 million francs in the Cannes casino while he was smoking a Hoyo de Monterrey panatela. He kept the remains of the cigar in a silver box. His cigar cutter, which had previously been owned by Lord Mountbatten, was eventually acquired by director Francis Ford Coppola.

WAUGH, EVELYN

Possibly the leading British novelist of the 20th century, and certainly of his generation, Waugh was an enthusiastic cigar smoker and *bon vivant*. The Partagas brand was mentioned in his greatest work, *Brideshead Revisited* (1945). His diary makes many references to cigar smoking – whether at home at Combe Florey, in Somerset, at White's Club in St James's or in restaurants such as Wiltons. He was often pictured smoking a cigar, and he smoked while he worked. His attitude to cigars was summed up by his comment, 'The most futile and disastrous day seems well spent when it is reviewed through the blue, fragrant smoke of a Havana.'

WELLES, ORSON

One of the greatest names in the history of cinema smoked cigars from the time his extraordinary career took off with *Citizen Kane* in 1941 (he was 26) until he died in 1985. He also smoked cigars in a number of movies including *Touch of Evil* (1958), which he also directed, and in which he played the unscrupulous, cigar-chomping cop, Hank Quinlan. The film also starred cigar lover Marlene Dietrich. Zino Davidoff recorded that Welles always demanded a box be opened before he bought it. 'If refused, he grumbles but buys the whole box anyway. He has never complained about his purchases.' The actor's favourite brand was Por Larranaga. Suitably, for a man of his eventual girth, he liked big cigars.

Left ORSON
WELLES

ZANUCK, DARRYL F.

The famous head of production at Twentieth Century-Fox was rarely photographed (unless on one of his polo ponies) without a cigar, and had an investment in a Vuelta Abajo plantation. He liked dark, full-bodied Colorado wrappers, on cigars such as the El Rey del Mundo Corona. He first started smoking cigars regularly in 1925 when, at the age of 23, he became head of production at Warner Brothers with a salary of $250,000 a year. He thought that smoking cigars (along with growing a moustache) would make him look older and give him a greater air of authority. The best cigar of the day, he thought, was the first one he lit in the evening. He would then chain-smoke them into the early hours while viewing rushes and poring over scripts. "I would rather die with a cigar in my mouth than boots on my feet," he said to his doctor after suffering a stroke. In *The Longest Day* (1962), his friend Robert Mitchum is seen sporting a cigar almost permanently during D-Day in his role as Brigadier-General Norman Cota.

Index

Page numbers in bold text indicate illustrations.

A

Adams, John Quincy, 20, 188
ashtrays, 174, **183**, **184**
Aztecs, 10

B

Bance, Jose, 94
Barthelemy, Auguste, 169, 188
Berle, Milton, 188
Bismark, Otto Von, 23, **188**
Bock, Gustavo, 17, 146, 174, 188–189
Bonaparte, Napoleon III, 189
Brazil, 126
Buck Duke's Tobacco Trust, 189
Burns, George, 189
Byron, Lord, 22, 189

C

Caine, Sir Michael, **189**
Cameroon, 37, 41, 127
Canary Islands, 30, 37, 90, 127, 139,
    140, 150, 193, 199
Cano, Tomas and Jose, 88
Carillo, Ernesto, 144
Cartier, 182
Caruso, Enrico, 189
Casa del Habano shops, 37
Castro, Fidel, 29, 189–190
Chaplin, Charlie, 24–**25**
Chase, Simon, 165
Christie's, 166
Churchill, Winston, **190**–191
Cifuentes, Ramon, 152, 191
cigar bands, 174
cigar boxes, **21**, 82, 174, **179**, **199**
cigar brands
    see also cigar manufacturers
    1492 humidors, 167
    Arturo Fuente, **128–129**, 169

Ashton, **130**
Avo, **131**, 168
Balmoral, **132**
Bauza, **132**
Belinda, 167, 199
Bolivar, 49, 50, **66–69**, 167
Cabinetta, 193
Cao, **133**
Casa Blanca, **134**
Chateau, 200
Cohiba, 30, 35, 49, 50, 58, **70–73**,
    165, 166, 167, 168, 174, 183,
    187, 194, 201
Cuaba, 31, **74**, 165, 166, 167
Cuesta Rey, **135**
Davidoffs, 31, **136–139**, 166, 167,
    168, 169, 182, 188, 194, 201
Diplomaticos, **75**
Don Alfredo, 193
Don Candido, 193
Don Diego, **140**
Don Nobodies, 35
Don Ramos, **141**
Don Tomas, **141**
Dunhills, **142–143**, 166, 167, 174,
    182, 188, 198
El Aguila de Oro, 17, 189
El Credito, **144**, 164
El Producto, 189
El Rey del Mundo, **76**, 174, 203
El Trovator, 190–191
Flor de Copan, **145**
Fonseca, **77**
Griffin, **145**
Henry Clay, 28, **146–147**, 188,
    189, 196, 197
Hoyo de Monterrey, 30, 50,
    78–81, 166, 167, 168, 174, 193,
    200, 202
Hoyo de Monterrey/Excalibur,
    148–149, 169, 174
H.Upmann, 30, 58, **82–85**, 167,
    168, 195
John Aylesbury, **150**
Jose L Piedra, **86**, 167
Joyo de Nicaragua, **150**
Juan Clemente, **151**
Juan Lopez, **87**
King Edward, 193
La Corona, 28, 193

La Escepcion, 167
La Flor de Cano, 58, **88**
La Gloria Cubana, **89**, 169
La Invicta, **151**
La Poeta, 189
Larranaga, 30, 196
Lords of England, 189
Macanudo, 44, 58, **152–155**, 167,
    169, 174, 191, 199
Malecon, 193
Mojito, 193
Montecristo, 28, 35, 75, **90–93**,
    165, 166, 167, 169, 188, 189,
    193, 201
Montecruz, 199
Padron, **156**, 169
Partagas, 30, 49, 50, **94–100**, 165,
    166, 167, 169, 181, 195, 196,
    199, 203
Paul Gamirian, **157**, 168
Petrus, **158**
Pleides, **158**
Por Larranaga, 58, **101**, 167,
    174, 203
Punch, 30, 58, **102–105**, 165, 169,
    199, 200
Quai d'Orsay, **106**
Quintero, **107**
Rafael Gonzalez, **108–109**, 197
Ramon Allones, 17, 49, **110–111**,
    165, 166, 174, 191
Ramon Cifuentes, 191
Romeo y Julieta, 30, **112–117**,
    165, 167, 169, 174, 184, 190,
    193, **200**
Saint Luis Rey, **118–119**, **179**, 201
San Cristobal, 31, **120**
San Luis Rey, 118
Sancho Panza, **121**
Santa Damiana, **159**
Siboney, 167
Te Amo, **159**
Temple Hall, 199
Toscani, 192, 201
Trinidad, **122–123**, 165, 167, 168
Upmanns, 188, 197
Valle, 197
Vegas Robaina, 31, **124**
Vegueros, **125**
Zino, **160–161**, 174, 192, 200

cigar cases, 174, **183**
cigar cutters, 174, **182**, **184**
cigar factories, 49–57
cigar handbags, **183**
cigar history, 8–37
cigar lighters, 174, **178**, **182**, **184**
cigar making, 38–61
    conditioning, 61
    grading, 61
    hand-finished, 57
    hand made, 40–61
    machine production, 28–29, 57–58
    packing, 61
    quality control, 58–61
    rolling, 29, 50–57, **60**
    tasting, 61
cigar manufacturers
    see also cigar brands
    Alfred Dunhill Ltd, 44, 90, 110,
        112, 140, 190
    Altardis, 37, 82, 90, 101, 118, 139,
        140, 143, 146, 158, 159
    American Tobacco, 112, 146
    Antonio Allones, 76
    Bernadino Rencurrel, 17
    Briones Montoto, 49, 118
    British American Tobacco, 140
    Cabanas, 112
    Carillo family, 142
    Carlos Torano, **179**
    Cifuentes family, 30, 89, 94,
        110, 152
    Consolidated Cigar, 37, 90, 146
    Cosme del Peso, 87
    Cubatabaco, 29, 118, 134, 140
    Davidoff, Zino, 80, 131, 136, 160
    El Laguito, 51, 70, 122, 136, 192
    Felipe Gregorio, 158
    Fernando Roig, 49, 102
    Francisco Donatien, 125
    Francisco Perez German, 49
    Fuente family, 128, 130, 132,
        145, 179
    General Cigar, 44, 49, 78, 94, 102,
        110, 138, 142, 148, 152, 164,
        191, 199, 200
    H. de Cabanas y Carbajal, 17
    Habanos SA, 37
    Henry Vane, **59**
    Hoyo de Monterrey, 102, 136,

        148, 190, 192, 199
    H.Upmann, 17, 49, 70, 82, 90,
        124, 198, 199
    Jose F. Rocha & Co, 66, 89
    Jose Marti, 49
    Juan Valle & Co, 102
    La Corona, 49, 102, 120
    La Gloria Cubana, 142
    M & N, 145
    Menendez family, 90, 94, 193, 199
    Menendez y Garcia, 30, 82, 90, 193
    Montecristo, 199
    Newman family, 145
    Oettinger, 131, 136, 143
    Palicio family, 30, 80, 102, 152
    Partagas, 49, 66, 70, 94, 191
    Piedra family, 86
    Pierre Lorillard, 15
    Por Larranaga, 28
    Ramon Allones, 110
    Rey del Mundo, 108, 121
    Romeo y Julieta, 49, 74, 76,
        108, 118
    SIETA, 37, 106, 158
    Tabacalera, 37, 132
    Tobacos Dominicanos, 143
    Tobacos Puros de Nicaragua, 150
    The Trust, 146
    Villazon, 148, 200
    Zamora y Guerra, 118
cigar: origin of word, 14
cigar scissors, 174, **182**
cigar shops, 171
cigar sizes, 64
    belicosos, 64
    Casa Blanca Jeroboam, 64
    Churchill, 64, 190
    corona, 57, 64
    double corona, 64
    especial, 64
    Esquisitos, 64
    figurados, 64, 74
    half corona, 199
    Lonsdale, 64, 197, 201
    Montecristo, 64
    panatela, 64
    parejos, 74
    petit corona, 57
    piramides, 57, 64
    robusto, 64

Royal Jamaica, 64
Sevillas, 190
Ten Downing Street, 64
torpedo, **56**
Trinidad, 37
Visible Inmeso, 193
cigar smoking: fashion and bans,
    13–14, **18–19**, 23–24, 35
cigar tubes, 82, 174
cigarettes, 24
cigars
    choosing, 170
    in films, 24–28
    in literature, 20–23
    publications, 35, 36, 122, 165
    smoking tips, 170
    and women, 36–37
Claridges Hotel, 35, 70, 152
Clay, Henry, 191
Clement, Jean, 151
Clinton, William Jefferson 'Bill', 20,
    191
Colette, Sidonie-Gabrielle, 169,
    191–192
Colibri, 182
Columbus, Christopher, 11–**12**
Connecticut, 15, 20, 41, 49, 127
Connecticut Shade, 15, 20, 41–42, 49
Conran, Sir Terence, 78
Coppola, Francis Ford, 192
Costa Rica, 37, 41, 127
Cuba, 14, 17–20, 28–35, 39–61

D

Davidoff shops, 136, **168**, 187,
    193, 197
Davidoff, Zino, 134, 160, 169,
    192, 200
De Vito, Danny, **186**
DeNiro, Robert, 192
Diaz, Juan Lopez, 87
Dominican Republic, 28, 30–31, 35,
    37, 41, 50, 61, 66, 77, 82, 89, 94,
    101, 110, 123, 126–159, 198–199
Dufy, Raoul, 192
Duke, James 'Buck', 28–**29**, 146
Dunhill, Alfred, 193
Dunhill shops, 140

E

Ecuador, 41, 127
Edward VII, King of England, 23–24, 193
Elgar, Sir Edward, 193

F

Farouk I, King of Egypt, 193
Fernandez, Rodriguez, 112
Florida, 28, 30, 60
Foch, Marshal Ferdinand, 193
Fonseca, F.E., 77
Freud, Sigmund, **193**
Frost, Sir David, 194
Fuschini, Enzina, **183**

G

Garcia, Jose Manuel, 90
Garcia, Pepe, 139
Garmirian, Paul, 157
Gener, Jose, 78
Germany, 150
Gonzalez, Carlos Izquierdo, 74
Gonzalez, Jose Manuel, 84
Gonzalez, Marquez Rafael, 108
Grant, Ulysses S., 20, 194
green cigars, 46
Grobet, Bernard, 143
Guevara, Che, 174, **194**

H

hand-made cigars, 40–61
Harrods, 37, 178, 184
Hart, Melbourne, 105
Havana cigars, 17–20
    see also Cuba; non-Havanas
    brands, 66–125
    cigar making, 40–61
Hemingway, Ernest, 194
Hitchcock, Sir Alfred, 90, 194–195
Honduras, 28, 30–31, 37, 41, 76, 78, 81, 102, 118, 121, 126–160, 192, 193

Hood, Thomas, 195
humidors, **172–173**, **176–177**, **180–181**, **184–185**
Hunter, John, 90
Hunters and Frankau, 66, 151, 165
Hussein, Saddam, 195

I

Indonesia, 37, 41, 127, 132
Infante, Guillermo Cabrera, 195
Italian cigars, 192, 201

J

J. Frankau & Co, 82
Jamaica, 28, 152, 190, 199
Jamaica Tobacco Co., 190
Joseph Samuel, 66

K

Kelner, Hendrik, 131, 136, 145, 157, 160
Kennedy, John F., 20, **195**–196
Kipling, Rudyard, 196

L

La Rochefoucauld, Duc De, 197
Lane, Martin, 181, 184
Larranaga, Ignacio, 101
Lenin, Vladimir Ilyich, 197
Levin, Robert, 130
Lewis, Bruce, **164**
Limoges, 183
Liszt, Franz, 197
Llaneza, Frank, 76, 102, 138, 149
Lonsdale, Lord, 108, 197
Lopez, Manuel, 102

M

Mallarme, Stephane, 22, **197**
Mann, Thomas, 197
Marti, Jose, 28, 29, 197–**198**
Marx, Groucho, 24, **27**, 198

Marx, Karl, 198
match boxes, 174
Maugham, (William) Somerset, 169, 198–199
Maya, 10
Mencken, Henry Louis, 199
Mexico, 28, 30, 37, 41, 126, 159
Michael de Keyser, 118
Morris & Elkan Ltd, 90
Musset, Alfred de, 22, 169, 199

N

Nathan Silverstone, 118
Netherlands, 132
Newman, Stanford, 135
Nicaragua, 37, 41, 126, 150, 156, 158, 198
Nicholson, Jack, 199
Nicot, Jean, 13
non-Havanas, 37
    brands, 126–161

O

Ohmstedt, Emilio, 76, 121
Ozgener, Cano A., 133

P

Padron, Jose O., 156
Palicio family, 30, 192, 199–200
Partagas, Don Jamie, 94
Peterson, 182
Piedra, Jose Lamadrid, 86
Putnam, Israel, 15, 200

Q

Quintero, Augustin, 107

R

Ravel, Maurice, 200
Reagan, Ronald, 134, 156
Rey, Angel La Madrid Cuesta, 135
Rey, Peregrino, 135

Rivera, Eduardo, 66
Robaina, Don Alejandro, 124
Robert Lewis, 17, 190
Robinson, Edward G., **26**
Ronson, 182
Rothschild family, 200
Rubinstein, Arthur, 200

S

Sahakian, Edward, 168
Sand, George, 169, 201
Schneider, Ernst, 134
Schwarzenegger, Arnold, 201
Scott, Ridley, 201
Seville, 14, 17
Sibelius, Jean, 201
Simpson's-in-the-Strand, 23
Sinatra, Frank, 201
S.T. Dupont, 182
Stendhal, 22, 201
stogie, 20

T

Taino Indians, 11–13, 74
Tamayo, Emilia, 122
Thackeray, Wiliam Makepeace, 169,
    201–202
Thackeray, William Makepeace, 22
tobacco
    ageing, 46, 49
    blending, 50, **52**
    Criollo, 29
    curing, 44, **47**, 49
    fermentation, 44, **47**, **48**, 49
    grading, 46
    growing, 40–44
    Habanenis, 29
    harvesting, 44, **45**
    leaves, 43
    rolling, 50–57, **60**
    stripping, 46
    Tabaco Negro Cubano, 29
Tobacco Trust, 28
Trollope, Anthony, 22, 202
Twain, Mark, 22–23, 202

U

Uvezian, Avo, 131

V

Van Dongen, Kees, 169, 202
Venezuela, 28

W

Wagner, Richard, **202**
Warhol, Andy, 174–175
Warner, Jack, 202–203
Waugh, Evelyn, 169, 203
Welles, Orson, **203**
Wynne, Gregory, 158

Z

Zanuck, Darryl F., 76, 169, 203

Acknowledgements and Thanks

Mark Acton; **Alamy Images**: 33; 41 **akg-images**: 10; 188 **Chris Barrass**; **Simon Chase**; **Jean Clarke**; **Corbis Picture Library**: 8; 11; 15; 16; 18; 21; 23; 25; 26; 29; 31; 32; 36; 38; 43; 45; 48; 56; 59; 60; 168; 195; 198; 202 **Rory Gill**; **Sarah Hannah**; **Michael Heizelight**; **Martin Lane**; **Bruce Lewis**; **Janelle Rosenfeld**; **Edward Sahakian**; **Werner Schmitz**